Journeying through Lent

with **New Daylight**

BRF
Ministries

 Ministries

15 The Chambers, Vineyard
Abingdon OX14 3FE
+44 (0)1865 319700 | brf.org.uk

Bible Reading Fellowship is a charity (233280)
and company limited by guarantee (301324),
registered in England and Wales

ISBN 978 1 85746 965 6
First published 2019
Reprinted 2022, 2024
10 9 8 7 6 5 4 3 2
All rights reserved

Acknowledgements
Scripture quotations marked with the following abbreviations are taken from the
version shown. Where no abbreviation is given, the quotation is taken from the
same version as the headline reference. NRSV: The New Revised Standard Version
of the Bible, Anglicised edition, copyright © 1989, 1995 by the Division of Christian
Education of the National Council of the Churches of Christ in the United States
of America. Used by permission. All rights reserved. NIV: The Holy Bible, New
International Version (Anglicised edition) copyright © 1979, 1984, 2011 by Biblica.
Used by permission of Hodder & Stoughton Publishers, a Hachette UK company.
All rights reserved. 'NIV' is a registered trademark of Biblica. UK trademark
number 1448790.

Every effort has been made to trace and contact copyright owners for material
used in this resource. We apologise for any inadvertent omissions or errors, and
would ask those concerned to contact us so that full acknowledgement can be
made in the future.

A catalogue record for this book is available from the British Library

Printed and bound in the UK

Contents

Luke 22–24: from upper room to Easter Day

BROTHER RAMON SSF

About the contributors

Helen Julian CSF was an Anglican Franciscan sister and a priest, serving her community as minister general from 2012 until her death in 2021. She wrote three books for BRF and contributed to BRF's *New Daylight* Bible reading notes and the Holy Habits resources on Fellowship.

Rachel Boulding was deputy editor of the *Church Times*, having previously worked at Church House Publishing, where she helped to produce the Common Worship materials. Before her death in 2017, she contributed regularly to BRF's *New Daylight* Bible reading notes.

Stephen Cottrell is archbishop of York and was formerly bishop of Chelmsford and bishop of Reading. He has written widely on evangelism, spirituality and discipleship.

Tony Horsfall is a freelance trainer and retreat leader. His recent BRF books include *Mentoring Conversations* (2020), *Deep Calls to Deep* (2021) and *Grief Notes* (2022). He contributes to BRF's *New Daylight* Bible reading notes.

Brother Ramon SSF was an Anglican Franciscan friar and a writer on everyday spirituality. His numerous books include *Praying the Jesus Prayer Together* (BRF, 2001) and *When They Crucified My Lord* (BRF, Centenary Classics edition, 2022). Brother Ramon died in 2000.

Introduction

SALLY WELCH

I have known my friend Julie for over 30 years. We met in a church crèche which we went on to lead, graduating to toddler services, then ordination training one after the other, and now we are both parish priests. We have shared issues with children, had discussions over church management, swapped ideas for Christmas plays and supported each other through the challenges and joys of parenting, ministry and all the other things which make up our everyday lives. We try to see each other regularly, but even if some months pass before we meet, each time we do it, it is as if we had only met yesterday. We know each other's weaknesses and gifts, triumphs and failures. We value our friendship.

The writers who are journeying alongside us in this Lent book are old friends of BRF. They have offered their wisdom and experience, their thoughts and reflections, to many readers through the years. Three of them are no longer with us, having made their final journey into eternity, but their words remain to comfort and challenge us as we look to those 40 days of prayer and study in preparation for the glorious event of Easter. The subjects which have been chosen are studies of some of the most important elements of our faith, and to each of these the writer brings their own unique interpretation. Helen Julian takes the theme of feasting and fasting beyond the narrow confines of eating or abstaining from food and explores generosity and self-control, choices and priorities. Rachel Boulding helps us to examine the radical nature of the beatitudes and apply their teaching to our own lives, while Stephen Cottrell unpacks the wisdom of Christ and carefully reveals its loving, sacrificial nature. Finally, as we head towards that most solemn of weeks, Tony Horsfall examines the love poem which is 1 Corinthians 13, before Brother Ramon gently but firmly leads us through Holy Week, knowing we must face the darkness before we can see the light.

I pray that these five writers – new to some of you, old friends to many – will prove to be valuable companions on the road to Easter. May their words encourage and support you, offering new ways of thinking and bringing new meaning to familiar passages so that you arrive at Easter refreshed and energised, ready to join in the cry: 'He is not here. He is risen!'

Sally AnnWelch

How to use this material in a group

This material can be used in a number of different ways by all sorts of groups. It can form the basis for a weekly Lent group or provide topics of discussion at Lent lunches or suppers. It can be used as conversation starters for groups that already meet, such as midweek fellowship groups, Mothers' Union meetings or men's breakfasts.

If a new group is beginning, it is a good idea to include refreshments with each meeting – some groups find an evening meal with discussion round the table very popular, while others feel that drinks and biscuits or cake are more appropriate. This kind of hospitality can break down barriers and introduce people to each other in a relaxed way, which in turn will lead to a livelier, more fruitful discussion.

Remember to provide prospective members of the group with booklets well before the beginning of Lent. The reflections begin before Ash Wednesday and they will provide a useful way into the first theme and style of writing before the meetings begin.

The group leader may or may not also be the group host. Either or both of these roles may be fixed for the whole of Lent or rotate among the group.

If the group leader and host are different people, they should liaise beforehand to ensure arrangements are in place, the time and date are fixed and refreshments are available.

Introduction Make sure each person has a copy of the booklet and that spares are available for those who do not. Introduce newcomers to the group and make them feel welcome. Remind everyone that they do not have to contribute to the discussion if they don't want to, but that conversation will be livelier if they do!

Opening prayer Use a prayer within the traditions of the group; this will help put people at ease, and those who are familiar with the traditions will lend confidence to those who are not. A song or hymn can be sung.

Discussion If the group is large, split into twos or threes to discuss reactions to the week's reflections. Allow time for each person to share, if they wish. If discussion is slow to start, suggest that each member offers one word or sentence that sums up their reaction.

Forum As one group, try to discern some themes that are common to most members. If it helps, write these down and circulate them among the group.

Reflection Each set of study questions relates to one specific day's reading. You may wish to read that day's reflection aloud together first. Then study the group questions, and spend some time in silence so that individuals can reflect on the theme personally. Come together to discuss the questions. Again, if the group is large it is helpful to split into smaller groups.

Plenary The leader draws together the themes arising from the discussion, and sees whether they mirror those from the week's reflections. Again, these can be noted for later distribution.

Prayer It can be helpful to begin your prayer time with silence, in order to meditate on the results of the discussion. This can be followed by open prayer. Be flexible, allowing time for each person to contribute if they wish.

Closing prayer.

Feasting and fasting

HELEN JULIAN CSF

Wisdom to choose

Luke 7:31–35 (NRSV)

'To what then will I compare the people of this generation, and what are they like? They are like children sitting in the market-place and calling to one another, "We played the flute for you, and you did not dance; we wailed, and you did not weep." For John the Baptist has come eating no bread and drinking no wine, and you say, "He has a demon"; the Son of Man has come eating and drinking, and you say, "Look, a glutton and a drunkard, a friend of tax-collectors and sinners!" Nevertheless, wisdom is vindicated by all her children.'

Reflection

'Some people are never satisfied,' you can almost hear Jesus say in exasperation. He has just healed the centurion's slave and the widow of Nain's son. He has named John the Baptist as a great prophet and God's messenger, preparing the way for the Messiah. Yet, many of the religious people, the Pharisees and the lawyers, refuse to accept either John or Jesus. They are, says Jesus, like spoilt, sulky children, who won't join in with the game their friends are playing, because it's always the wrong game.

So, John comes, living an ascetic life, living in the wilderness and fasting, and they accuse him of being possessed. Jesus comes, eating and drinking, often with the less-respectable people, and they accuse him of being a greedy drunkard. God, though, has sent both John and Jesus. Each is honouring God in the way he lives, and each has his own followers.

Certainly Jesus had fasted and would fast again, but, for now, it was right to feast, to share meals with those who were not usually invited to feasts. John's ministry and Jesus' ministry complement each other, yet each is criticised for not doing what the other does.

'For everything there is a season... a time to mourn, and a time to dance' (Ecclesiastes 3:1, 4). We need the wisdom to know what is right for this season and time. Jesus, the wisdom of God (1 Corinthians 1:24), leads his children so we know when it is time to fast or to feast, to mourn or to dance.

Jesus, wisdom of God, make me sensitive to your leading and ready to follow wholeheartedly.

HELEN JULIAN CSF

Generous God

Isaiah 55:1–3a (NRSV)

Ho, everyone who thirsts, come to the waters; and you that have no money, come, buy and eat! Come, buy wine and milk without money and without price. Why do you spend your money for that which is not bread, and your labour for that which does not satisfy? Listen carefully to me, and eat what is good, and delight yourselves in rich food. Incline your ear, and come to me; listen, so that you may live.

Reflection

Visiting India, I was struck by the number of people selling water by the roadside. A very small sum bought a glass of water with a squeeze of lime. Imagine having to buy your water by the glassful or, even worse, being too poor to pay even the tiny price of a drink. Especially in a hot country, that really is being in want.

In this parable, God is a water seller like no other. The familiar cry, drawing attention to what he has to sell, is transformed. This water seller is giving away his stock free to anyone who needs it. His stock is not only water, but also bread; and not only bread and water, the necessities of life, but also wine and milk, the luxuries.

In Isaiah's parable, God is not only the street seller, but also the rich benefactor. Someone wishing to be generous would buy up the entire stock of a water carrier or a baker and order him to distribute it free. God does this not once but continuously. His generosity is unmatched.

There is still more. Not content with supplying free both the necessities of life and the luxuries, he goes on to promise the gift of life itself. Bread and water, wine and milk – these may be necessary and pleasurable, but they are not enough. If all our energies are focused on them and what they stand for, we will ultimately not be satisfied. Only in coming to God and listening to his word – the Word, Jesus – will we receive the greatest gift of our generous God: 'I came that they may have life, and have it abundantly' (John 10:10).

On what do I spend my money and my labour?

HELEN JULIAN CSF

Show me

Joel 2:1, 2, 12–14 (NRSV, abridged)

Blow the trumpet in Zion; sound the alarm on my holy mountain! Let all the inhabitants of the land tremble, for the day of the Lord is coming, it is near... a great and powerful army comes... Yet even now, says the Lord, return to me with all your heart, with fasting, with weeping, and with mourning; rend your hearts and not your clothing. Return to the Lord, your God, for he is gracious and merciful, slow to anger, and abounding in steadfast love, and relents from punishing. Who knows whether he will not turn and relent, and leave a blessing behind him, a grain-offering and a drink-offering for the Lord, your God?

Reflection

'Don't talk of love, show me,' sang Eliza Doolittle in *My Fair Lady*. Here are God's people, facing a great calamity, a mighty army advancing on them, and this is God's doing – 'the day of the Lord is coming'. Recognising this, the people want to demonstrate to God their sorrow for their sins, their unfaithfulness, everything that has brought this day on them. Just talking about it won't do. Like Eliza Doolittle, God wants something more concrete. Fasting and weeping and mourning are ways of showing God their love and sorrow. They back up the words and strengthen them.

But even such dramatic action, though more effective than words alone, is not enough. The call is to repent 'with all your heart'. For the Hebrews, this did not necessarily mean 'with all your feeling'. The heart represented intellect and will as much as emotions, so perhaps 'with all your heart' could be translated as 'with purpose and resolve'. The heart must also be torn, broken, as mourners tore their clothes as a sign of grief.

The heart, broken open, with a real resolution to change, can then truly turn, return, repent and come back into a relationship with the gracious and merciful God. This return is celebrated with feasting, grain and drink offering to God, who waits with steadfast love to feast with his people.

**What authentic ways can I find of showing God
my penitence for sin?**

HELEN JULIAN CSF

Glory to God

Matthew 6:16–18 (NRSV)

'And whenever you fast, do not look dismal, like the hypocrites, for they disfigure their faces so as to show others that they are fasting. Truly I tell you, they have received their reward. But when you fast, put oil on your head and wash your face, so that your fasting may be seen not by others but by your Father who is in secret; and your Father who sees in secret will reward you.'

Reflection

The key word here is 'whenever'. Jesus takes it for granted that his disciples will give alms, pray and fast, and here he tells them how to go about these practices. 'How to' is only the beginning, though – far more important, and far more demanding, is 'why'.

'Beware of practising your piety before others in order to be seen by them' (6:1). The almsgiver should not be accompanied down the street by a servant blowing a trumpet. The one who prays should go into their room and shut the door. When Jesus' disciples fast, it should be as a personal act of devotion between them and God. No one else should be able to tell. They should look and act as they normally do.

Does this contradict what Jesus said just a little earlier in the sermon on the mount – 'Let your light shine before others, so that they may see your good works' (5:16)? No, because, again, the motivation is all-important. Verse 16 goes on to say, 'And give glory to your Father in heaven.' God must be the focus of almsgiving, prayer and fasting, and God's reward is the only one the disciples long for. It's a good test of our Lent resolutions this Ash Wednesday.

Our natural human tendency to want others to think well of us is a problem for the spiritual life. It makes us self-conscious, aware of being seen. The great saints, Francis among them, seem to have escaped this. Francis responded directly to God, praying, singing, dancing, weeping, fasting or feasting. He was so intoxicated with God that he was oblivious of others' opinions of him. His eyes were fixed on God and God's was all the glory.

God of glory, help me to fix my eyes only on you.

HELEN JULIAN CSF

Hungry for God

Luke 2:36–38 (NRSV)

There was also a prophet, Anna the daughter of Phanuel, of the tribe of Asher. She was of a great age, having lived with her husband for seven years after her marriage, then as a widow to the age of eighty-four. She never left the temple but worshipped there with fasting and prayer night and day. At that moment she came, and began to praise God and to speak about the child to all who were looking for the redemption of Jerusalem.

Reflection

'She's never out of the church' may be a compliment or rather less than one. We may perhaps think of a lonely old woman, with no life of her own. Anna, however, who 'never left the temple', is not one of those.

Only seven women in the whole of the Old Testament are named as prophets. Anna's long life of worship in the temple in Jerusalem – the centre of the world for God's people – made her especially sensitive to the signs of God's presence. Like Simeon, she had waited faithfully for the coming of the Messiah. So, when the child Jesus was brought into the temple, she recognised him and knew that this was cause for rejoicing.

Her worship included both prayer and fasting and, in the scriptures, these two usually belong together. Fasting from food in order to focus more completely on God has a long pedigree. Of course, it isn't automatically successful. I have a friend who became so desperate for chocolate while on a fasting retreat that he walked eight miles over mountain paths to buy a bar. 'It was all that was good in the universe,' he recalled. Fasting is not an automatic passport to opening up in us a hunger for God. Rather, it may make it humiliatingly clear where our hunger really lies.

Perhaps Anna, too, found it hard in the beginning. However, she persevered, perhaps for as long as 60 years, and, in the end, her hunger was satisfied. Like Simeon, her eyes saw God's salvation and her soul rejoiced.

**What am I hungry for? How might fasting, from food
or something else, help me to focus more on God
this Lent?**

HELEN JULIAN CSF

True fasting

Isaiah 58:6–8a (NRSV)

Is not this the fast that I choose: to loose the bonds of injustice, to undo the thongs of the yoke, to let the oppressed go free, and to break every yoke? Is it not to share your bread with the hungry, and bring the homeless poor into your house; when you see the naked, to cover them, and not to hide yourself from your own kin? Then your light shall break forth like the dawn, and your healing shall spring up quickly.

Reflection

My mother recalls that my sister and I would burst in from school saying, 'Do you know, it's not fair,' before we'd even taken our coats off. Then would follow some saga of injustice. The instinct for fair play is a very deep one.

God's people think that he isn't treating them fairly. Just before this passage, they are complaining, 'Why do we fast, but you do not see? Why humble ourselves, but you do not notice?' (58:3). We are doing all the right things, God. Why are you not rewarding us as we deserve?

God's reply is devastating. Your fasting is worthless if it is accompanied by oppression, quarrelling and violence (58:3–4). Fasting like this is only an outward show, an empty ritual. Then God details what must accompany fasting if it is to be pleasing to him. Justice, liberation, compassion and care for neighbour are what God chooses. These are what please him, these are what will cause him to hear his people when they call to him.

The prophets call their hearers to 'do justice, and to love kindness' (Micah 6:8). God cares passionately about justice, but we cannot bargain our way into his favour with our fasting or our beautiful services or our long prayers. These have their place, but God looks for justice and compassion, expressed in the very concrete details of our lives, as well.

Merciful God, you loose the bonds of injustice and let the oppressed go free: give us the will to share our bread with the hungry and give shelter to the homeless poor, for thus your glory shall be revealed, through Jesus Christ our Lord. Amen

HELEN JULIAN CSF

The feast of the kingdom

Luke 14:12–14 (NRSV)

He said also to the one who had invited him, 'When you give a luncheon or a dinner, do not invite your friends or your brothers or your relatives or rich neighbours, in case they may invite you in return, and you would be repaid. But when you give a banquet, invite the poor, the crippled, the lame, and the blind. And you will be blessed, because they cannot repay you, for you will be repaid at the resurrection of the righteous.'

Reflection

When I moved to the East End of London, I knew what kind of church I wanted to join. I would look for somewhere fairly large and successful where, for a time, I could just sidle in and out and not be asked to do anything. I ended up at a tiny congregation, at that time without a priest, where I was immediately pressed into service, but in the end I was grateful.

Although small, the congregation came from an amazing range of backgrounds. On an average Sunday, there would be traditional working-class East Enders, a retired teacher or two from the leafier suburbs, me from Scotland, two or three older people from the Caribbean, a young family from the Far East, perhaps a Latin American. The priest who soon came to care for the parish was Anglo-Indian. I used to look around at the Eucharist and think, 'This is what the kingdom looks like.' People from all classes and ages and all parts of the world, united by nothing at all except their desire to worship God.

This is one of Jesus' parables of the kingdom. The feast of the kingdom is not like most of our parties – a time to enjoy our friends or perhaps impress our neighbours or colleagues, knowing that next it will be their turn to invite us. The feast of the kingdom is, as theological commentator Dennis McBride says, 'for people who need food because they are hungry, who need company because they are outcast, who need rejoicing because they know sadness, who need sharing because they are isolated in their sickness'.

**What would it mean in my life and in my church
to follow Jesus' advice to his host?**

HELEN JULIAN CSF

Week 1 | Group study questions

Isaiah 55:1–3a (Monday)

1 At the start of Lent, what do you thirst for or feel you lack?

2 When have you experienced true, memorable generosity from others?

3 What do you think it means to 'come to the waters' and 'buy and eat'? How do we do this?

4 What does abundant life look like, and how can we be truly satisfied?

5 How can we reach out to those who are hungry and thirsty, in any sense? What can you commit to doing this week?

Bread in the wilderness

Matthew 4:1–4 (NRSV)

Then Jesus was led up by the Spirit into the wilderness to be tempted by the devil. He fasted for forty days and forty nights, and afterwards he was famished. The tempter came and said to him, 'If you are the Son of God, command these stones to become loaves of bread.' But he answered, 'It is written, "One does not live by bread alone, but by every word that comes from the mouth of God."'

Reflection

This is a story full of echoes. The wilderness, the number 40, stones and bread – all take the reader back to the Old Testament. The voice of the tempter takes Jesus back to the voice at his baptism – 'This is my Son, the Beloved' (Matthew 3:17). Jesus goes into the wilderness as the people of Israel did after their liberation from Egypt (Deuteronomy 8:2), and fasts for 40 days, as did both Moses (Exodus 34:28) and Elijah (1 Kings 19:8). For Jesus, as for these others, it is a time of testing – 'testing you to know what was in your heart' (Deuteronomy 8:2). The people of Israel failed the test. They doubted God, rebelled against Moses, complained about the food that God provided and even regretted their liberation from slavery.

Jesus does not fail despite all this. He neither takes on the tempter in his own newly realised power, nor does he despair of God's help. He looks back into the tradition out of which he comes and draws from it words to express his trust in God, words from Deuteronomy 8.

William Barclay says, 'We are tempted through our gifts.' It's a sobering thought. We are accustomed to thinking of our weaknesses as places where we may face temptations, but our strengths and gifts can tempt us to the wrong sort of autonomy. The devil seems to taunt Jesus: '*If you are the Son of God*' – prove it to me. Jesus does prove it, but not in a show of power. His obedience to the word of God is a better proof than that. It is also his bread: 'My food is to do the will of him who sent me' (John 4:34).

Where do my gifts lead me into temptation?

HELEN JULIAN CSF

The king's feast

Isaiah 25:1, 4, 6–8 (NRSV, abridged)

O Lord, you are my God; I will exalt you, I will praise your name; for you have done wonderful things… For you have been a refuge to the poor, a refuge to the needy in their distress… On this mountain the Lord of hosts will make for all peoples a feast of rich food, a feast of well-matured wines, of rich food filled with marrow, of well-matured wines strained clear. And he will destroy on this mountain the shroud that is cast over all peoples, the sheet that is spread over all nations; he will swallow up death for ever. Then the Lord God will wipe away the tears from all faces, and the disgrace of his people he will take away from all the earth, for the Lord has spoken.

Reflection

Perhaps it isn't today's idea of a healthy diet, but the feast of 'rich food filled with marrow' and the best wines were the caviar and champagne of their day. This is a description of a coronation banquet, the celebration of the enthronement of God as king. He will reign 'on Mount Zion and in Jerusalem' (Isaiah 24:23) and his reign marks the final defeat of death. Unlike many of the kings of the time, God is a king who brings liberation, who is on the side of the poor, so his coronation banquet is open to everyone, not just the rich and powerful.

St Francis called himself 'the herald of the great king'. He went about preaching the gospel, depending on others to supply his needs. One day, he and Brother Masseo went out to beg. Masseo, who was tall and good-looking, was given many good pieces of bread, even whole loaves. Francis, however, small and ragged, received only a few scraps, ends of loaves, dry and unappetising. They met outside the town at a fountain to eat. Masseo was aware of how little they had – no plates, knives, tablecloth, servants – but Francis was joyful and praised God for his provision. 'We have this bread as a gift,' he said, 'and water to drink, and a stone by the fountain as our table. Everything is given by God, and so it is a great treasure.'

Rich food and the best wines or bread and water – where God is acknowledged as the giver, everything is feast.

Generous God, help me to feast on your gifts today.

HELEN JULIAN CSF

Us and them

Isaiah 58:9b–11 (NRSV)

If you remove the yoke from among you, the pointing of the finger, the speaking of evil, if you offer your food to the hungry and satisfy the needs of the afflicted, then your light shall rise in the darkness and your gloom be like the noonday. The Lord will guide you continually, and satisfy your needs in parched places, and make your bones strong; and you shall be like a watered garden, like a spring of water, whose waters never fail.

Reflection

Fasting from food can leave us feeling empty, hungry, for a short time, but the fast ends and once again we can satisfy our hunger. Some hungers, though, can only be satisfied at the expense of others. Our fast from these should be permanent.

'The pointing of the finger, the speaking of evil' – a graphic description of the natural human tendency to divide our world into 'us' and 'them'. Then 'they' can be blamed, even made scapegoats, for the problems we perceive. This can nourish 'us' – we define our identity in opposition to 'them' and feel superior and secure; it builds us up.

God's people always wrestled with this temptation. They had been chosen by God and they had the law – surely they were superior to the nations around them because of this? The prophets had to constantly remind them that their calling to be God's people was not because they deserved it, but purely because of God's covenant love. Increasingly, they also spoke of God's desire for all the people of the world to come within this covenant.

Gratitude, trust in God and a desire to serve others, not superiority and separation, were the appropriate responses to God's choice of his people. If they fasted from the easy satisfaction of 'us' and 'them', then God would supply their real needs. He would always be with them to guide them and would build up their strength. Their dry places, their thirst, would be reliably watered and their darkness turned to light.

**Covenant God, teach me to satisfy my hungers
only in knowing and serving you. Amen**

HELEN JULIAN CSF

Going beyond ourselves

Acts 13:1–3 (NRSV)

Now in the church at Antioch there were prophets and teachers: Barnabas, Simeon who was called Niger, Lucius of Cyrene, Manaen a member of the court of Herod the ruler, and Saul. While they were worshipping the Lord and fasting, the Holy Spirit said, 'Set apart for me Barnabas and Saul for the work to which I have called them.' Then after fasting and praying they laid their hands on them and sent them off.

Reflection

I wonder if Barnabas and Saul wanted to be 'sent off'? Perhaps they were very happy at Antioch. They had been there for a year and the church was growing. They had a recognised role there, numbered among the prophets and teachers. Setting off on a missionary journey around the eastern Mediterranean may have been the last thing on their minds.

God, however, had other ideas. He used a time of worship and fasting to speak to the church. Fasting has often been used along with prayer to help in discerning God's will and making decisions. Learning that it's possible to do without something that is usually central to life can have a very liberating effect. We begin thinking, 'I couldn't survive without…', but discover that 'actually I can'. That can free us to wonder what else might be possible.

Doing something new and challenging can have the same effect. I always hated sport at school and would have said, 'I'm no good at that sort of thing,' but now I practise aikido, a martial art. Every time I pass a grading and get my new coloured belt, I'm amazed to find myself doing this. It challenges me in other areas where I might want to say, 'I'm no good at that sort of thing.'

As Christians, we draw not only on our own as yet unrecognised resources, but on God's, whose Holy Spirit is always surprising us and challenging us to move beyond the safe and the known, 'for nothing will be impossible with God' (Luke 1:37).

**God of the impossible, lead me beyond myself
into your future.**

HELEN JULIAN CSF

Excuses, excuses

Luke 14:16–23 (NRSV, abridged)

Then Jesus said to him, 'Someone gave a great dinner... he sent his slave to say... "Come; for everything is ready now." But they all alike began to make excuses. The first said to him, "I have bought a piece of land, and I must go out and see it; please accept my apologies." Another said, "I have bought five yoke of oxen, and I am going to try them out; please accept my apologies." Another said, "I have just been married, and therefore I cannot come." So the slave returned and reported this to his master. Then the owner of the house became angry and said to his slave, "Go out... and bring in the poor, the crippled, the blind, and the lame... so that my house may be filled."'

Reflection

The slave had already come round once, to announce the feast, and those invited had given their acceptance. Now the feast was ready and he went again to tell them that it was time to come. Only the important people were treated like this. However, even though the host had done everything that he should, each guest now had something more important to do. They put their own activities first and so insulted the host by going back on their acceptance.

So the host sends to ask others – the unimportant and those not usually invited to feasts. Only the physically whole could participate fully in Jewish worship, but here the blind and the lame are invited along with everyone else.

No one is excluded from the feast of the kingdom except by their own choice. God is the host, who will not start the feast until his house is filled with willing guests. When those first invited refused, he could have simply enjoyed the feast on his own or, in anger, cancelled it altogether, but he does not. God wants company at his table, where the feast is always ready.

It's easy to put off responding to God's gracious invitation. Other things seem more urgent and surely God will go on inviting? Yes, God's patience far outruns our procrastination, but each invitation is for 'now' and will not come again. Today's feast will not still be available tomorrow.

**What excuses do I use to avoid sitting down
to feast with God?**

HELEN JULIAN CSF

Bought at a price

1 Corinthians 6:12–14, 19–20 (NRSV)

'All things are lawful for me', but not all things are beneficial. 'All things are lawful for me', but I will not be dominated by anything. 'Food is meant for the stomach and the
stomach for food', and God will destroy both one and the
other. The body is meant not for fornication but for the
Lord, and the Lord for the body. And God raised the Lord
and will also raise us by his power… Or do you not know
that your body is a temple of the Holy Spirit within you,
which you have from God, and that you are not your
own? For you were bought with a price; therefore glorify
God in your body.

Reflection

Paul has often been used to support a misunderstanding of
Christianity, which denigrates and devalues the body. His
opposition of 'spirit' and 'flesh' (Romans 8:1–13; Galatians
5:16–25) has been used to support a negative view of the
physical. The less attention given to the body the better, so
fasting and other harsh treatments are virtuous.

This passage is a corrective to that. The body is 'a temple of
the Holy Spirit' and so is to be treated with respect, as a

place in which God can be glorified as much as in our mind or heart or spirit. Fasting may be a means of doing this, but so may eating sensibly or taking appropriate exercise.

What Paul does warn against is being 'dominated by anything'. Lent is a good opportunity to examine ourselves – what do I believe I cannot do without? It may be food or, more likely, particular kinds of food (not many people are addicted to lettuce). It may equally be television, social media, alcohol, shopping, constant background music, a particular relationship. None are bad in themselves – 'all things are lawful' – but if they dominate my life, then they are no longer beneficial.

Fasting from anything that has too high a place in my priorities could be a way of returning God to the centre of my life, acknowledging that I am not my own.

**Lord, help me to remember that I belong to you,
and let me seek your glory in all that I do.**

HELEN JULIAN CSF

An 'in-between' time

Mark 2:18–20 (NRSV)

Now John's disciples and the Pharisees were fasting; and people came and said to him, 'Why do John's disciples and the disciples of the Pharisees fast, but your disciples do not fast?' Jesus said to them, 'The wedding-guests cannot fast while the bridegroom is with them, can they? As long as they have the bridegroom with them, they cannot fast. The days will come when the bridegroom is taken away from them, and then they will fast on that day.'

Reflection

John's disciples and the Pharisees and their disciples were still waiting, waiting for the coming of the Messiah. They were still in the 'in-between' time, between the promise and its fulfilment. It was not yet time for the feast.

Jesus' disciples, even at this early stage in the gospel, however, have come to believe that he is the Messiah, the promised one. For them, there is ample cause for celebration and so fasting would be as inappropriate as it would be at a wedding.

The time will come when the bridegroom will leave them and then, Jesus recognises, the time of feasting will be over. At the last supper, keeping the Passover with his disciples, he vowed to abstain until the coming of the kingdom (Luke 22:14–18).

So, where are we now? Should we fast or feast? The wedding has taken place, but the bridegroom is no longer with us. We are in another 'in-between' time. With the Passion and resurrection of Jesus, the reign of sin is over and the kingdom has begun, so we can feast. However, the final victory has not yet been realised, so there is still cause for fasting.

In the Eucharist, both these perspectives are present. The broken bread and wine, outpoured, look back to Jesus' broken body and the blood he poured out on the cross. A meal shared with friends gathered round a table looks forward to the banquet of the kingdom, the final celebration of the redemption and liberation at the end of the age.

In the space between the 'now' and the 'not yet' of the kingdom, we can both fast and feast.

**Help me to live creatively in the 'now',
but not lose sight of the 'not yet'.**

HELEN JULIAN CSF

Week 2 | Group study questions

1 Corinthians 6:12–14, 19–20 (Friday)

1 Where do you feel at risk of being 'dominated' by things that are not beneficial?

2 Can we identify things to give up or fast from for a time? This could be in our church, in our culture or in our personal lives.

3 Fasting and feasting can be seen as opposite sides of a coin. As we fast from certain things, how can we feast in other ways? Ideas might include sharing a meal or Communion as a group or organising an outreach meal.

4 What will you commit to this week, and how can we support one another in this?

5 In silence, pray for those you know who are struggling with behaviours that are 'lawful' but not 'beneficial'.

The sermon on the mount

RACHEL BOULDING

The world turned upside down

Matthew 5:1–6 (NRSV)

When Jesus saw the crowds, he went up the mountain; and after he sat down, his disciples came to him. Then he began to speak, and taught them, saying: 'Blessed are the poor in spirit, for theirs is the kingdom of heaven. Blessed are those who mourn, for they will be comforted. Blessed are the meek, for they will inherit the earth. Blessed are those who hunger and thirst for righteousness, for they will be filled.'

Reflection

Matthew opens his collection of some of Jesus' most important teaching with the beatitudes. Luke's version appears differently: it is shorter and there isn't the same stress on our actions (Luke 6:20–49). The first half of each describes what life is like now; the second promises hope, which might be fulfilled only in the next world.

The beatitudes turn this world's values on their head. On one level, they take despised and dreaded things and suggest that good will come from them: 'Blessed are those who mourn, for they will be comforted' (v. 4). The beatitudes were the main gospel reading when one of my friends took his final vows as a monk. The monastic life of renunciation, sharing and obedience represents the reversal of the world's worship of money, sex and personal choice.

This gives the beatitudes an elusive quality. They are like good poetry – always suggesting further depths of meaning. It's important, too, that they are not commands: 'Blessed are the meek' doesn't mean the same as 'You must be meek'. Instead, they build a picture of the type of people God thinks are special. God doesn't necessarily want everyone to go around desperately trying to be humble and unassertive – that doesn't work. Rather, it's saying that God values genuinely unassuming people and won't walk all over them in the way that people in the world generally do.

So, these first four beatitudes don't mean that we have to try to make ourselves poor in spirit, mourners or meek (though hungering after righteousness could be helpful). Rather, we should be aware that God cherishes people like this. When we get the chance, we can try to value these qualities in others and cultivate them in ourselves.

Father, help me to learn true meekness.

RACHEL BOULDING

Perhaps the pushy aren't so blessed

Matthew 5:7–12 (NRSV)

'Blessed are the merciful, for they will receive mercy. Blessed are the pure in heart, for they will see God. Blessed are the peacemakers, for they will be called children of God. Blessed are those who are persecuted for righteousness' sake, for theirs is the kingdom of heaven. Blessed are you when people revile you and persecute you and utter all kinds of evil against you falsely on my account. Rejoice and be glad, for your reward is great in heaven, for in the same way they persecuted the prophets who were before you.'

Reflection

People have sometimes tried to convey the revolutionary qualities of the beatitudes by imagining a worldly version as a contrast: 'Blessed are the rich: they will have everything they want' and 'Blessed are the pushy: they will get their own way'. The strange thing is that we all know secretly in our hearts that only God's values can satisfy our deepest needs, that worldly values are hollow. Money can't buy us love, and not many people really want to be thought of as pushy.

So we know that it is actually better to be merciful, because we all need mercy sometimes; and to be pure in heart, because we all have such mixed motives; and to be peace-makers, because drawing up battle lines isn't the way of the cross.

The final two beatitudes – outlining blessings on those persecuted for righteousness and for the Lord's sake – are even harder to fathom. As we saw yesterday, it's not a case of looking to be persecuted but, instead, reminding ourselves of the ultimate values: what really matters.

All this adds up to a picture of the people ignored and even despised by the world, but whom God cherishes. We can glimpse this sometimes in communities, such as the monastery that my friend was joining, the L'Arche community, where learning-disabled people live alongside others, and those churches where everyone is valued and personal holiness is matched by active concern for others. Many saw this quality in the six Melanesian Brothers in the Solomon Islands who, in 2003, went unarmed to help another Brother who had been kidnapped. There was no guile in them, but they were murdered for their faith.

**What small action can I do today to reflect
God's kingdom?**

RACHEL BOULDING

Glowing with God's grace

Matthew 5:13–16 (NRSV)

'You are the salt of the earth; but if salt has lost its taste, how can its saltiness be restored? It is no longer good for anything, but is thrown out and trampled under foot. You are the light of the world. A city built on a hill cannot be hidden. No one after lighting a lamp puts it under the bushel basket, but on the lampstand, and it gives light to all in the house. In the same way, let your light shine before others, so that they may see your good works and give glory to your Father in heaven.'

Reflection

If we put the beatitudes into practice, we become the salt of the earth. We don't accept the world's values, so we stand out and give a distinctiveness to the whole. We're like light, which makes a difference to the whole room. We don't have to be flashed about, just put on a candlestick to shine steadily. Even a tiny flame enables people to see in the dark.

We have to tread the fine line between being different from the world (not swallowed up by its values, not losing our savour) and being proper salt and light, which enhances whatever it comes into contact with – not overwhelming it, but bringing out the flavour or colour of what is already there. It's not for us to judge the world (that's what only God can do), but to draw out its good side.

Accordingly, our faith shouldn't be focused on ourselves. It's not about self-improvement, to make us wonderful people. Instead, it's about what we can do for others, for all people, whom God loves. Together we can build up a kingdom of people who turn towards God and find their true fulfilment in him.

As Hubert van Zeller wrote (*Considerations*, Templegate, 1974), Jesus has invited us to enter into his light: 'He has asked us not merely to reflect it, but to be it.' Then, it's not glitzy and superficial. Think of your favourite film star – you might describe their performance as 'luminous', when they truly inhabit a part. Imagine yourself glowing with God's grace like that.

Meanwhile, just a grain or two of salt can add a certain extra something. We can each make a difference, however small.

What have I ever done to enhance others' lives?

RACHEL BOULDING

With God all things are possible

Matthew 5:17–18, 20 (NRSV)

'Do not think that I have come to abolish the law or the prophets; I have come not to abolish but to fulfil. For truly I tell you, until heaven and earth pass away, not one letter, not one stroke of a letter, will pass from the law until all is accomplished... For I tell you, unless your righteousness exceeds that of the scribes and Pharisees, you will never enter the kingdom of heaven.'

Reflection

This is a vital piece of teaching, that corrects some danger-ous misunderstandings – ones that have persisted into the 21st century. Jesus hasn't come to reject the Jewish law. When some Christians imply that the law can be ignored, as if we're above all that now, they are going against Jesus' specific instructions. Paradoxically, their very concern with the law and response to it reveals how much they are still bound by rules rather than thinking about what lies behind them, as Jesus does.

What Jesus is actually saying is that God's kingdom is so completely different from our earthbound ideas that we can barely imagine it. The fulfilment of his law goes beyond all this and does so in extraordinary ways, but does not cancel it out.

Jesus is the fulfilment of the law in himself, so he would hardly then trivialise it. As a good and observant Jew, he cared about it and would never want to see it scorned. Yet, he doesn't just say that we should obey the law, but that we should outdo even its great teachers in following it. We've got to be even keener than the most devout people. As we saw with the beatitudes, God's ways are so far from our ways that we can only hope to catch something of his vision to inspire us. His ways are ideals set before us, not strictures of impossible perfection that we can only fail to achieve as we try to carry them out.

So Jesus exaggerates. When he wants to tell us that no one can do this by human effort, he surely means that we must realise all the more why we need God. We ought to sense how dependent we are.

'Who then can be saved?'… 'With man this is impossible; but with God all things are possible'
(Matthew 19:25–26, NIV).

RACHEL BOULDING

God's ways are not our ways

Matthew 5:21–24 (NRSV)

'You have heard that it was said to those of ancient times, "You shall not murder"; and "whoever murders shall be liable to judgement." But I say to you that if you are angry with a brother or sister, you will be liable to judgement; and if you insult a brother or sister, you will be liable to the council; and if you say, "You fool", you will be liable to the hell of fire. So when you are offering your gift at the altar, if you remember that your brother or sister has something against you, leave your gift there before the altar and go; first be reconciled to your brother or sister, and then come and offer your gift.'

Reflection

Jesus continues his exaggeration of exactly how righteous we should be. One of the curious things about it is the mixture of extreme idealism and common-sense wisdom. Some of it seems so down-to-earth that no one could disagree with it, but other parts seem so heavenly minded as to be of no earthly use.

Are we really not supposed to get angry? Shouldn't we be angry at cruelty and suffering, or angry as Jesus himself was with the abuses of the moneychangers in the temple, and as God was in the Old Testament over Israel's sins? Surely this is all part of Jesus' pushing things to extremes to show how completely we need to immerse ourselves in God's ways and just how different they are from ours. We need to lose our box-ticking approach to good and bad, which so often has an edge of 'I'm better than you'. Instead, we should embrace a larger vision of God's whole kingdom.

Such an approach might mean that, in the end, we do great things, but it has to start first with the attitudes behind these actions. So, we need to look at what leads us into sins such as murder and examine the anger in our own hearts. Then we can see that there is not such a great dividing line between law-abiding religious people and thieves, murderers and rapists. We are all human and all need God's mercy.

'For my thoughts are not your thoughts, nor are your ways my ways, says the Lord' (Isaiah 55:8).

RACHEL BOULDING

A call to wholeness

Matthew 5:27–30 (NRSV)

'You have heard that it was said, "You shall not commit adultery." But I say to you that everyone who looks at a woman with lust has already committed adultery with her in his heart. If your right eye causes you to sin, tear it out and throw it away; it is better for you to lose one of your members than for your whole body to be thrown into hell. And if your right hand causes you to sin, cut it off and throw it away; it is better for you to lose one of your members than for your whole body to go into hell.'

Reflection

The wild exaggeration continues. Have you ever heard of Christians mutilating themselves like this? If the Archbishop of Canterbury preached such a sermon today, he might be carried off for psychological investigation!

Clearly, Jesus is talking about ideals, not concrete realities. One way to look at this might be to compare the way he is going beyond mere keeping to the rules to what is called virtue ethics. These emphasise the importance of basic character rather than simply what is done or said. This approach encourages people to develop virtues, such as, here, respect for others – not seeing them as objects for personal gratification (sexual or otherwise) – and self-control and discernment about personal sins.

Virtue ethics can be discussed in a purely secular way, but it has parallels with Jesus' vision of the kingdom. He is calling us to be people of integrity.

So this passage isn't saying that it is wrong to have lustful thoughts, but savouring them and letting them lead us into sin is. The Greek words have a sense of moving towards something. It's something we should try to resist.

These words also suggest how much the kingdom should matter to us. We know that it's not supposed to be just a delightful hobby or even a way of life that makes us feel fulfilled, although we often seem to behave as if that is all it is. Instead, Jesus says it's like a pearl of great value, in that it means so much to us that we dispense with everything else we have in order to have only this (Matthew 13:46).

Is there anything that stops me from following Jesus wholeheartedly? What about money, the way I think of others and my desire for an easy life?

RACHEL BOULDING

Beyond plain speaking to integrity

Matthew 5:31–37 (NRSV, abridged)

'It was also said, "Whoever divorces his wife, let him give her a certificate of divorce." But I say to you that anyone who divorces his wife, except on the ground of unchastity, causes her to commit adultery; and whoever marries a divorced woman commits adultery. Again, you have heard that it was said to those of ancient times, "You shall not swear falsely, but carry out the vows you have made to the Lord." But I say to you, Do not swear at all, either by heaven, for it is the throne of God, or by the earth, for it is his footstool… Let your word be "Yes, Yes" or "No, No"; anything more than this comes from the evil one.'

Reflection

In contrast to the earlier parts of the sermon on the mount, these would seem like straightforward instructions. So, why do many, if not most, Christians go against these clear commands from our Lord? How can we possibly justify divorce on the grounds of, for example, violence? How can we defend swearing on the Bible in court?

Jesus seems to be pointing towards what Paul later described as the contrast between the spirit and the letter

(2 Corinthians 3:6). He knows that divorce is definitely not a matter of a simple certificate. It is a devastating ripping apart of one flesh – like a death. Our western society, however, has gone to the other extreme and tries to pretend that it is not a great problem.

Clearly whole books could be (and have been) written about this, so what follows are only suggestions, in the context of the sermon on the mount as a whole. These chapters suggest a wider approach to how we ought to behave – broader than just looking at particular rules. They seem to be saying that we should cultivate healthy attitudes and the values of the kingdom in every way we can. We should search for God's values, not our natural selfish wishes: 'strive first for the kingdom of God' (Matthew 6:33). If we try to see situations as God sees them, we will surely be merciful to others and generous concerning their problems, rather than taking it on ourselves to judge them.

**Pray for those in troubled and broken relationships.
Think of one thing you might do to support them.**

RACHEL BOULDING

Week 3 | Group study questions

Matthew 5:13–16 (Tuesday)

1 As a group, come up with a definition of a person who is 'the salt of the earth'. What would they be like?

2 How close to this definition do you feel you are at the moment?

3 How can we be salt and light – as a group, as individuals, as a church – in our communities?

4 How can we 'draw out the good side' of the world?

5 What 'small difference' will we commit to making this week?

Dare to surrender your goods

Matthew 5:38–42 (NRSV)

'You have heard that it was said, "An eye for an eye and a tooth for a tooth." But I say to you, Do not resist an evildoer. But if anyone strikes you on the right cheek, turn the other also; and if anyone wants to sue you and take your coat, give your cloak as well; and if anyone forces you to go one mile, go also the second mile. Give to everyone who begs from you, and do not refuse anyone who wants to borrow from you.'

Reflection

Theologian Jane Williams suggests that Jesus tells us here to be 'foolishly generous to others', to allow ourselves 'to be treated unfairly by the greedy and the powerful and the anxious because we know that nothing they can do can actually dispossess us'.

Some of the people who are most at home in the kingdom are like this. Certainly not meek and mild, they have the type of fearlessness that doesn't mind about more blows landing on their other cheek. They sit so lightly to their own comfort and long-term security that they freely give away their belongings. Would I have anything like the guts to do that? I don't think so.

All the same, these words give me a vivid image of the sort of person I should try to be. I shouldn't think myself generous just because I give to others from my loose change and spare possessions, but should make sacrificial donations.

It's hard to think of anyone who is so free from the all-encompassing snare of worldly goods that they ever behave like this. Perhaps another friend in the religious life, a Franciscan friar, comes closest. He certainly has more freedom, having given up his 'right to choose'. He has relinquished the objects that the rest of us hug to ourselves as a comfort blanket – the gratification that comes from choosing our own clothes, work, companions and possessions. Sometimes it seems as if these things are all that we have to define ourselves, but thinking in this way means that we are missing out. If only we would dare to surrender them, we might find that there are greater blessings.

Of course, there is one person who lived this philosophy perfectly: Jesus himself. In his suffering and death, he turned the other cheek and didn't demand any 'rights'.

**Father, help me to realise that my true security
lies with you.**

RACHEL BOULDING

The perfect approach to good and bad

Matthew 5:44–46, 48 (NRSV)

'But I say to you, Love your enemies and pray for those who persecute you, so that you may be children of your Father in heaven; for he makes his sun rise on the evil and on the good, and sends rain on the righteous and on the unrighteous. For if you love those who love you, what reward do you have? Do not even the tax-collectors do the same?… Be perfect, therefore, as your heavenly Father is perfect.'

Reflection

How much further can Jesus push this? He has already sketched the most special people in the kingdom as being the despised, persecuted and dispossessed. Now he sums it up by saying 'Be perfect.' That's all? Should be a doddle…

Of course, we know that we can never be perfect, but that doesn't mean we should give up. The required attitude could be summarised as both 'If a thing's worth doing, it's worth doing well' and 'If a thing's worth doing, it's worth doing badly.' We need to keep trying afresh every morning. Being 'perfect' doesn't mean being sinless, either. The

Greek word is *teleios*, which is more like finished, whole or having integrity.

The big point is that we're not doing this on our own. Jesus calls us to be perfect like our heavenly Father. We're in a relationship to a loving parent who can help us. This is a Father who sends sun and rain on good and bad alike. That is what we have to try, too – loving dodgy people as well as nice ones and not expecting anything back. If we truly have the Spirit of Jesus within us, we'll find ourselves doing this as a matter of course, not because it's sensible or practical (it isn't either).

Some Christians wouldn't approve of this – they'd call for a boycott on sinners. Certainly God isn't having much regard for purity here, but what he is saying is that the impulse to draw boundaries of who's in and who's out of God's love isn't religious at all. It's just another way of the world – a grubby human desire to bolster ourselves up as the in-crowd by picking on other people as the unclean crowd.

If God sends rain on the just and the unjust, can we ever judge who might fall into either category?

RACHEL BOULDING

Depending on God

Matthew 6:1–4 (NRSV)

'Beware of practising your piety before others in order to be seen by them; for then you have no reward from your Father in heaven. So whenever you give alms, do not sound a trumpet before you, as the hypocrites do in the synagogues and in the streets, so that they may be praised by others. Truly I tell you, they have received their reward. But when you give alms, do not let your left hand know what your right hand is doing, so that your alms may be done in secret; and your Father who sees in secret will reward you.'

Reflection

Matthew groups together various religious activities – almsgiving and, in the verses following, prayer and fasting – not just to recommend them, but to outline how they should be carried out. He stresses that all these activities should be done in secret.

This is about more than just avoiding showing off (though spiritual pride worms its way into the most intimate places of our hearts). It is about not doing the right thing for the wrong reason. If we're being religious in outward ways for the sake of the reward of heaven and praise from others, what does that make us? Nasty little creeps, always looking away from the matter in hand to check on what other people think and thinking that we can fool God.

This is a long way from the wholehearted love we were asked to have for people in yesterday's reading. It's easy to fall into the trap of keeping our faith and what is really important to us in separate compartments. We can so easily choose to be religious in one tiny way and limit our faith to our own choices, then act as if we don't depend on God.

The fact is, we do depend on God for everything, and giving, prayer and fasting should remind us of that. It should also remind us that we're part of the wider world that God loves. He cherishes the poor and the hungry, who don't have any choice about fasting and have little to give away. We're all in this together and all equally loved by God. How can we fail to help and love the people God loves?

Father of us all, fill every corner of my being.

RACHEL BOULDING

Your Father knows you

Matthew 6:5–8 (NRSV)

'And whenever you pray, do not be like the hypocrites; for they love to stand and pray in the synagogues and at the street corners, so that they may be seen by others. Truly I tell you, they have received their reward. But whenever you pray, go into your room and shut the door and pray to your Father who is in secret; and your Father who sees in secret will reward you. When you are praying, do not heap up empty phrases as the Gentiles do; for they think that they will be heard because of their many words. Do not be like them, for your Father knows what you need before you ask him.'

Reflection

As we saw yesterday, it's all too easy to think of such faults as belonging to someone else – perhaps a pompous church member or, historically, particular groups of first-century people. These words, though, are directed squarely at us now.

Have you ever caught yourself lingering in prayer, wanting to appear spiritual? Even in private, have you ever piled up elegant phrases, pleased with your own fluency or the number of people and situations you're praying for? God knows what we want regardless of how we present our pleas and perhaps smiles at our pretensions. We should present ourselves to him without any dissembling. Yet again, Jesus stresses that it is our underlying attitudes that are important, not how we seem or what we actually do as we pray.

Praying without 'empty phrases' is demonstrated in the old story of the person who explains that they pray simply by sitting in church quietly alone: 'I look at God and he looks at me.' I've met people who assume that individual prayer is always like this and are surprised that the story comes as a revelation to others, releasing them from thinking up elaborate rhetoric.

Often, however, we need something – perhaps words, the way we sit or kneel, a picture or a candle – to ease us into that state where we become aware of God's power and love. President Theodore Roosevelt used to take his guests outside to see the stars after grand diplomatic dinners. He would gaze up and remind them how vast the distances were in space. Then he would end, 'Do we feel small enough now?'

What helps you to become aware of God's presence?

RACHEL BOULDING

Beneath God's overarching love

Matthew 6:9–15 (NRSV)

'Pray then in this way: Our Father in heaven, hallowed be your name. Your kingdom come. Your will be done, on earth as it is in heaven. Give us this day our daily bread. And forgive us our debts, as we also have forgiven our debtors. And do not bring us to the time of trial, but rescue us from the evil one. For if you forgive others their trespasses, your heavenly Father will also forgive you; but if you do not forgive others, neither will your Father forgive your trespasses.'

Reflection

At last, after all the teaching about general approaches to prayer, Jesus gives us some actual words. But, of course, they don't tell us everything. As we've heard before, we need to be wholehearted about them, praying them from deep inside with our total being.

It's useful to read the Lord's Prayer as part of the sermon on the mount, seeing how it puts into practice the themes of the beatitudes and other teachings. It begins with 'Our Father', stressing the family relationship between all of us and our loving creator. This is where all our yearning springs from, both between people and for God. This is where our prayer and fasting and giving have their source.

Yet, this loving Father is also the holy one, far above the sins of the world. He is our hope for life in heaven in the future, though he is intimately bound up with us now. This hallowedness is what should make us realise that the meek and those who grieve for the state of the world are correct. Being poor in spirit before almighty God is only right. We should pray that the kingdom – the world of the beatitudes and selfless giving – is brought about. In this kingdom, we have our needs, but these are part of the pool of others' needs. It's a reciprocal situation. We forgive others and they forgive us, all under the loving rule of God. We can only pray for his overarching love to protect us from the judgement to come as we acknowledge our debt to and dependence on him. We are all sinners, each and every one of us, and we need to approach others with the same attitude of mercy that we hope for ourselves, rather than presume to judge them.

Pray this version of the Lord's Prayer, lingering over each phrase and thinking how it applies to your situation today.

RACHEL BOULDING

Where is your treasure?

Matthew 6:19–21, 24 (NRSV, abridged)

'Do not store up for yourselves treasures on earth, where moth and rust consume and where thieves break in and steal; but store up for yourselves treasures in heaven, where neither moth nor rust consumes and where thieves do not break in and steal. For where your treasure is, there your heart will be also... No one can serve two masters... You cannot serve God and wealth.'

Reflection

I once found my beautiful cardigan had some holes in it where a moth had got at it. Thankfully, it was mendable, but finding it in that state made me unduly upset, not least because it was partly my fault. I have some lovely clothes – more than my grandmothers could have dreamed of and more than I need – but am I grateful to God for such luxury every time I get dressed? Not really. Could I give them away tomorrow to those who need them more than I do? Not without feeling a terrible loss.

I read about someone who had all his possessions stolen. They'd been packed in a removal van, and he had only the clothes he stood up in. He was devastated, but family and friends rallied round and gave him things and cash to buy more. When he began to acquire new goods, though, he felt he'd lost something – some of the freedom of not possessing anything.

Most of us store up treasures, whether they be clothes, a house or a pension fund, but of course it's the underlying attitude to them that matters. Could we manage without them? When we get a sense of how much we rely on such things, even love them, we glimpse how much we can and should depend on God. We can see how our whole self is wrapped up in these possessions when, really, it ought to be wrapped up in God.

My words and thoughts do both express this notion,
That Life hath with the sun a double motion.
The first is straight and our diurnal friend,
The other hid and doth obliquely bend.
One life is wrapped in flesh, and tends to earth.
The other winds towards Him, whose happy birth
Taught me to live here so.
George Herbert (1593–1633)

RACHEL BOULDING

Knowing we're part of God's kingdom

Matthew 6:25, 28–29, 32–33 (NRSV, abridged)

'Therefore I tell you, do not worry about your life, what you will eat or what you will drink, or about your body, what you will wear. Is not life more than food, and the body more than clothing?... Consider the lilies of the field, how they grow; they neither toil nor spin, yet I tell you, even Solomon in all his glory was not clothed like one of these... Your heavenly Father knows that you need all these things. But strive first for the kingdom of God and his righteousness, and all these things will be given to you as well.'

Reflection

Jesus develops yesterday's theme in this rightly celebrated passage. Reading it within the sermon on the mount, we can see that he is emphatically not judging the many people who have died for lack of food and clothing. As Jane Williams puts it, 'Are we to assume that they somehow failed to concentrate sufficiently on the kingdom, and so were punished?... I think not.'

Instead, he is urging us to focus on what is really important and turn away from our anxieties. Yes, there are economic interests that are keen to keep us buying stuff that we don't need, but surely the real problem is our selfish hearts. We don't recognise what will be truly satisfying and, instead, palm ourselves off with inferior junk, whether it's food, clothes, possessions or feel-good experiences. We cling on to things that can't ever meet our needs. We're like children who want to eat only sweets – no wonder we become sick at heart.

What can we do to realign ourselves with what God has designed to fulfil us? Jesus says simply that our priority should be the kingdom of God and God's righteousness. It sounds straightforward enough, but, of course, it's not that easy. We so easily wander away in our thoughts and can't manage this from our own reserves of strength, but at least we can start each day by setting it within the framework of God's kingdom.

As you begin the day, try to imagine what you're going to do in a fresh light. Seek God in your actions, the people you're going to meet and your reactions to events.

RACHEL BOULDING

Week 4 | Group study questions

Matthew 5:44–46, 48 (Monday)

1 What injustices are on our hearts this evening? Share these on Post-it notes or together on a larger piece of paper. These could be for ourselves or others we know of.

2 Honestly, do you feel 'finished, whole, having integrity'? If not, where are the gaps?

3 What can we do about these?

4 Are there particular situations where we need to pray for the ability to forgive?

5 Which 'enemies' will we commit to praying for this week?

Jesus' wisdom in Luke

STEPHEN COTTRELL

The better part

Luke 10:38–42 (NRSV)

As they went on their way, [Jesus] entered a certain village, where a woman named Martha welcomed him into her home. She had a sister named Mary, who sat at the Lord's feet and listened to what he was saying. But Martha was distracted by her many tasks; so she came to him and asked, 'Lord, do you not care that my sister has left me to do all the work by myself? Tell her then to help me.' But the Lord answered her, 'Martha, Martha, you are worried and distracted by many things; there is need of only one thing. Mary has chosen the better part, which will not be taken away from her.'

Reflection

Be honest: is there anyone who hasn't occasionally found this story a little irritating? Of course Mary has chosen the better part – Jesus says so – but we still have a sneaking sympathy for Martha. While her sister sits at Jesus' feet, she does all the work! Most of us can think of occasions where we have been the Martha and have looked with thinly veiled exasperation at rather too many people who, casting themselves in the role of Mary, have failed to pull their weight. So, let's get this clear from the beginning: there is work to be done, and Jesus does not mean that we should sit around in prayer and contemplation while others do our share. We need Marthas and Marys and we must each discover the Martha and the Mary inside ourselves.

There is a time for everything, says the book of Ecclesiastes (3:1–8): a time for work, a time for rest and a time for prayer. Wisdom is about staying close to Jesus in all three. We need to make Jesus our guide, not Mary. She does the right thing in this situation, but so does Martha in others. After all, it is Martha who welcomes Jesus into the house in the first place. Let us welcome Jesus into our lives through these scriptures that we shall be exploring together and learn wisdom for our daily lives.

Holy Spirit, guide my life this week. Enable me to stay close to Jesus and to learn his wisdom for my life.

STEPHEN COTTRELL

Lord, teach us to pray

Luke 11:1–2 (NRSV)

[Jesus] was praying in a certain place, and after he had finished, one of his disciples said to him, 'Lord, teach us to pray, as John taught his disciples.' He said to them, 'When you pray, say: Father, hallowed be your name. Your kingdom come.'

Reflection

'Teach us to pray.' That is what the disciples ask Jesus, and it is where Christian wisdom begins and ends. 'The fear of the Lord is the beginning of knowledge' (Proverbs 1:7). We learn this fear and knowledge of God when we live our lives in communion with God, which is nurtured by prayer, a prayer that is made possible by what God has done for us in Jesus Christ. He is the one in whom we pray; he is the one who teaches us the way of prayer. Prayer is God's work in us.

So Jesus teaches his friends. He says to them, 'Pray like this': 'Father, hallowed be your name. Your kingdom come', though in the version of the Lord's Prayer from Matthew's gospel (the one we may say ourselves each day), Jesus also adds 'Your will be done, on earth as it is in heaven' (Matthew 6:10). These three together – holding God's name holy, seeking God's will and working for God's kingdom – are the heart of prayer. It is not about feverishly hectoring God with all the stuff we think he should be attending to, but about giving him honour and praise, seeking his will for our lives and for the world, and using the words of Jesus to shape our mind and will.

Prayer is not just intercession. It is not about our trying to change God's mind. It is praise and adoration. It is about being open to God changing ours. This is the way of Christian wisdom.

We can do no better than making the Lord's Prayer our prayer. Many great spiritual writers have commented that if we could just say the Lord's Prayer once, really meaning it, then we would be holy. Give it a try; it will take a lifetime, but, by happy coincidence, that's exactly how much time each of us has.

**Jesus, teach me to pray. Teach me your prayer,
and do your will in me.**

STEPHEN COTTRELL

Give us what we need

Luke 11:3–4 (NRSV)

'Give us each day our daily bread. And forgive us our sins, for we ourselves forgive everyone indebted to us. And do not bring us to the time of trial.'

Reflection

Once we have prayer round the right way, then life is round the right way. First of all, prayer is not about what we say to God; it is about what God says to us. Thus, it begins with the hearty praises we offer to God in the first three clauses of the Lord's Prayer. In the rightness and the goodness of this relationship we can then ask God anything. So it is that the Lord's Prayer continues with three humble petitions where we ask God for our most basic needs – provision for each day, sins to be forgiven (and the grace to forgive others) and for God to save us from the time of trial.

Once again, we find that Jesus' own words enable us not just to say the prayer but also to discover what we really want. Other spiritual writers have said that our own deepest desire *is* the will of God. The trouble is that most of the time we are not aware of what we truly want – we are only aware of ourselves at a very superficial level – but this prayer reveals what we really need and shapes our deepest longings.

We live in a world that always wants more. We are imprisoned by our own possessions and our obsession with getting more. We nurse grievances and grudges against our neighbours. Meanwhile, so many of our current economic woes are caused by debt on a grand scale and an inability to share with others. In a world of plenty, millions still starve. The problem is simple: we do not know the wisdom of God. We put ourselves first. We expect too much. We ask for what we do not need.

What a different world it would be if we could simply learn to ask for daily bread, daily forgiveness and nothing more, then be satisfied with it.

God, give me what I need and save me from asking or craving for more. Forgive me and help me to forgive others.

STEPHEN COTTRELL

Persevere

Luke 11:5–9 (NRSV)

[Jesus] said to them, 'Suppose one of you has a friend, and you go to him at midnight and say to him, "Friend, lend me three loaves of bread; for a friend of mine has arrived, and I have nothing to set before him." And he answers from within, "Do not bother me; the door has already been locked, and my children are with me in bed; I cannot get up and give you anything." I tell you, even though he will not get up and give him anything because he is his friend, at least because of his persistence he will get up and give him whatever he needs. So I say to you, Ask, and it will be given to you; search, and you will find; knock, and the door will be opened for you.'

Reflection

The wisdom of Jesus comes through stories as much as sayings. Many of what we today call parables could just as easily be called riddles or puzzles. They need to be worked out; each answer leads to another question. There is never a point where you can say, 'I've got it now.' That is because, ultimately, the wisdom of Jesus is Jesus himself. Remember the first words of the Lord's Prayer? 'Our Father'. That is not

God as we expected. Instead, he is a Father to us; he is ours; we can have relationship with him.

That relationship is made possible through Jesus, and this is the greatest wisdom of Christian scripture: Jesus is not just a teacher, not just a philosopher; he is God's wisdom enfleshed. So, as this playful little story puts it, be persistent. Ask. Search. Knock. This wisdom is instantly available through relationship with God in Jesus. You do need to work at it, but receiving it is not dependent on your work. It is given freely: 'received in one great gulp of grace', as the third-century saint Cyprian of Carthage put it. What you need to do is work out what it means for your life. That is the subject of a lifetime's learning. There will always be more to know and apply.

Jesus, help me to persevere in the school of your love, that I might learn from you.

STEPHEN COTTRELL

Asking for the right things

Luke 11:11–13 (NRSV)

'Is there anyone among you who, if your child asks for a fish, will give a snake instead of a fish? Or if the child asks for an egg, will give a scorpion? If you then, who are evil, know how to give good gifts to your children, how much more will the heavenly Father give the Holy Spirit to those who ask him!'

Reflection

We return again to the issue of asking for the right things, having our will refined. This is a point Jesus wants to labour. God knows you; God wants to give you what you need. Wisdom comes from him, so stop looking in the wrong places. Stop asking for the wrong things.

Unfortunately, what we need is not always the same as what we want. We do not always ask for fish or eggs: sometimes snakes and scorpions seem rather more beguiling. We hanker after what we should not have, what we know to be wrong. Sin is compelling and attractive; they do not call it temptation for nothing. If there were not so many seductions at hand, being chaste would be easy, fidelity a cinch.

If we allow ourselves to be shaped by God's wisdom, we will learn to desire and ask for the right things. This will not happen quickly or easily – it is part of that lifetime of discipleship where our stubborn wills are slowly shaped so that they conform to the will of God. As Jesus says, 'If you then, who are evil, know how to give good gifts to your children, how much more will the heavenly Father give the Holy Spirit to those who ask him!' (v. 13). That is the other great promise of the Christian faith: God will give us the Spirit, whom we need more than anything, because he will bring and instil the wisdom of Jesus in our lives. He will be God's work in us, his gift to us. The Spirit will bring forgiveness, perseverance, patience, self-control. With these we will learn what is good for us.

Heavenly Father, show me what I need and help me to desire it. Give me the Spirit, so that I may grow in the way of Christ.

STEPHEN COTTRELL

Saying 'yes' to God

Luke 11:27–28 (NRSV)

While [Jesus] was saying this, a woman in the crowd raised her voice and said to him, 'Blessed is the womb that bore you and the breasts that nursed you!' But he said, 'Blessed rather are those who hear the word of God and obey it!'

Reflection

Sometimes this passage can be read as Jesus giving his mother a bit of a put-down. Far from it! Jesus says that the one who is blessed is the one who hears the word of God and obeys it. If there is one person who exemplifies this obedience it is Mary, for, right at the beginning of the gospel story in Luke (1:38), she is the one who responds to the angel's strange and disturbing offer with absolute faithfulness: 'Here am I, the servant of the Lord; let it be with me according to your word.' Her cousin Elizabeth says of her, 'Blessed is she who believed that there would be a fulfilment of what was spoken to her by the Lord' (1:45). In other words, Mary is blessed not just because she bore the Christ but also because she 'hears the word of God and obeys it'.

We could go further and say that without her cooperation with the will of God, the Christ could not have come. God does not force himself on anyone, certainly not the virgin Mary and not in the incarnation. Heaven waits on earth's response, and Mary's 'yes' to God was the turning point of human history.

It is the same today. God will not force himself on any of us. He waits for our response, and we are blessed not because of any earthly mark of upbringing or pedigree (God is not impressed by our estimates of greatness), but because we too hear and respond to God's word and, by doing so, are incorporated into God's household. It is our being united with God's will that makes us part of God's family, brothers and sisters of Christ. Mary is therefore a model of Christian discipleship, one who teaches us how to receive and bear the wisdom of God that is Jesus Christ.

Heavenly Father, like Mary, teach me to say 'yes' to your word.

STEPHEN COTTRELL

Turning around

Luke 11:29–32 (NRSV)

When the crowds were increasing, [Jesus] began to say, 'This generation is an evil generation; it asks for a sign, but no sign will be given to it except the sign of Jonah. For just as Jonah became a sign to the people of Nineveh, so the Son of Man will be to this generation. The queen of the South will rise at the judgement with the people of this generation and condemn them, because she came from the ends of the earth to listen to the wisdom of Solomon, and see, something greater than Solomon is here! The people of Nineveh will rise up at the judgement with this generation and condemn it, because they repented at the proclamation of Jonah, and see, something greater than Jonah is here!'

Reflection

An obvious next question is, 'What do we do to receive this wisdom?' The answer is paradoxical. It cannot be earned or learned; it arises from our relationship with God. It is a free gift, but it must be consciously received, unwrapped and applied. That takes a lifetime of learning, which is where repentance comes in. Repentance is not the precondition for receiving God's wisdom, but it is a very necessary part of our ongoing response to God, whereby his image and likeness – his wisdom and his ways – are formed in us. 'The people of Nineveh will rise up at the judgement with this generation and condemn it, because they repented at the proclamation of Jonah,' says Jesus, 'and see, something greater than Jonah is here!' (v. 32). That which is greater than Jonah is the presence of Jesus himself, who is not just the one who calls us to repentance, but also the one through whom we are forgiven and reconciled to God.

The biblical word for repentance is *metanoia* – literally, 'turned around'. It is not just saying sorry for the things we do wrong, but a complete reorientation of life. Once we see the wisdom of God's way, we cannot help but recognise the waywardness of our own. That is the wisdom which is greater than Solomon's. It is not about our own insightful cleverness, but joyful obedience to God's directing.

Holy Spirit, redirect me.

STEPHEN COTTRELL

Week 5 | Group study questions

Luke 11:1–2 (Monday)

1 When do you feel closest to God in prayer? Alone or with others? In a formal or informal setting? When speaking aloud or in silent contemplation? When using liturgy or other familiar prayers, or just voicing our thoughts to our Father?

2 'Hallowed be your name.' How do we do this? What might we do that does not hallow God's name?

3 'Your will be done.' How do we know? What are the ways in which we can discern this?

4 'Your kingdom come.' As a group, try to picture this, and commit to one action this week that might bring God's kingdom closer.

5 Spend some time together praying through each phrase of the Lord's Prayer.

Let there be light

Luke 11:33–36 (NRSV)

'No one after lighting a lamp puts it in a cellar, but on the lampstand so that those who enter may see the light. Your eye is the lamp of your body. If your eye is healthy, your whole body is full of light; but if it is not healthy, your body is full of darkness. Therefore consider whether the light in you is not darkness. If then your whole body is full of light, with no part of it in darkness, it will be as full of light as when a lamp gives you light with its rays.'

Reflection

The image of a brightly burning lamp was much more powerful to a world without electricity. We take light for granted, but Jesus spoke to people who knew total darkness in a way that we do not. He uses the image of light again and again to describe his ministry and presence: 'I am the light of the world. Whoever follows me will never walk in darkness but will have the light of life' (John 8:12). He also uses it to describe the ministry of his disciples, who received the light from him: 'You are the light of the world. A city built on a hill cannot be hidden' (Matthew 5:14).

It is in this sense that Jesus speaks here, inviting his followers to consider carefully their response to his light. Is what you think to be light actually darkness? Do you need to turn again to God and let him illuminate your life? One thing is for sure: when we invite Jesus to be our light, he dispels all darkness and shines vividly within us so that our lives shine with the same illumination that we see in him.

Quoting the story of creation, where the first thing God creates is light, Paul puts it brilliantly when he writes, 'For it is the God who said, "Let light shine out of darkness", who has shone in our hearts to give the light of the knowledge of the glory of God in the face of Jesus Christ' (2 Corinthians 4:6).

Lord Jesus, shine on me. Illuminate my life and shine through me. Let your light in me illuminate the world.

STEPHEN COTTRELL

Doing the right thing

Luke 11:37–41 (NRSV)

While [Jesus] was speaking, a Pharisee invited him to dine with him; so he went in and took his place at the table. The Pharisee was amazed to see that he did not first wash before dinner. Then the Lord said to him, 'Now you Pharisees clean the outside of the cup and of the dish, but inside you are full of greed and wickedness. You fools! Did not the one who made the outside make the inside also? So give for alms those things that are within; and see, everything will be clean for you.'

Reflection

Now we get down to some of the nitty-gritty application of this wisdom. The Jewish people had all sorts of laws and ritual customs that shaped everyday life and helped create their identity as a people. The Pharisees are shocked when they see Jesus ignoring them. That does not mean Jesus thinks the law is unimportant, but he does react strongly against the fastidious application of complicated rituals when the heart of the law is ignored. Taking great care to wash the outside of a cup when your inner being is corrupted by greed and wickedness is not the way of God. Clean yourself first, is the message of Jesus.

We may live in a far more relaxed sort of society when it comes to the rituals that shape everyday life, but what matters is the inner motivation. An inner cleanliness of motive and desire is the gift of God's grace and forgiveness, refining our minds and wills so that our everyday actions, however small, will be done in service to God and to others. This way of approaching life is sometimes called 'practising the presence of God' – that is, living every moment as if in the very presence of God and, therefore, offering every thought and action to God. It is the fruitful outworking of Christian wisdom and the sign that Christian faith has become Christian life.

Wise and loving God, help me to know your presence with me every day. May my actions serve your glory and work for the building of your kingdom in the world.

STEPHEN COTTRELL

Facing conflict

Luke 12:8–12 (NRSV)

'And I tell you, everyone who acknowledges me before others, the Son of Man also will acknowledge before the angels of God; but whoever denies me before others will be denied before the angels of God. And everyone who speaks a word against the Son of Man will be forgiven; but whoever blasphemes against the Holy Spirit will not be forgiven. When they bring you before the synagogues, the rulers, and the authorities, do not worry about how you are to defend yourselves or what you are to say; for the Holy Spirit will teach you at that very hour what you ought to say.'

Reflection

Following in the way of Jesus leads to conflict. The world is very good at rejecting wisdom, especially wisdom that challenges the innate self-centredness of the human heart.

Towards the end of this chapter, Jesus says, 'I came to bring fire to the earth' (v. 49), and, in Matthew's gospel, 'Do not think that I have come to bring peace to the earth; I have not come to bring peace, but a sword' (Matthew 10:34). These are hard sayings. They do not contradict the central truths of the Christian faith that, as Paul says, through Christ, 'God was pleased to reconcile to himself all things' (Colossians 1:20), but we are living though the birth pangs of this new reality. Consequently, we will find ourselves in conflict with those earthly powers and principalities that are always bent on the destruction of what is good.

After all, Jesus himself was beaten and crucified, and he asks us to carry a cross (Luke 9:23). Hence, in our passage today, Jesus does not say '*if*' they bring you before the authorities (v. 11), but '*when*'. There is a sober acknowledgement that following Jesus will mean difficulty, but there is also comfort: 'The Holy Spirit will teach you at that very hour what you ought to say' (v. 12). Notice, however, that this wisdom is not delivered in advance: it is when the hour comes that the Holy Spirit will be at hand. Just trusting in God's provision when and where we need it is wisdom that we could all usefully learn.

Holy Spirit, teach me to trust in your provision.

STEPHEN COTTRELL

Treasure in heaven

Luke 12:16–21 (NRSV)

Then [Jesus] told them a parable: 'The land of a rich man produced abundantly. And he thought to himself, "What should I do, for I have no place to store my crops?" Then he said, "I will do this: I will pull down my barns and build larger ones, and there I will store all my grain and my goods. And I will say to my soul, Soul, you have ample goods laid up for many years; relax, eat, drink, be merry." But God said to him, "You fool! This very night your life is being demanded of you. And the things you have prepared, whose will they be?" So it is with those who store up treasures for themselves but are not rich towards God.'

Reflection

Now here is a story. We have looked quite a bit at the subject of wisdom in Luke's gospel, but only had one story. This is unusual, because Jesus is the great storyteller. So much of his wisdom is given in stories, not statements. Also, Luke's gospel is, arguably, the gospel with the greatest stories in it! This, in turn, reveals an important truth about truth: it cannot be pinned down.

The truth about Jesus is the truth about a person, and it is learned through a relationship. That is why the stories themselves are puzzling and challenging. They are either like this one – very obvious and therefore very disturbing – or else enigmatic and perplexing so that you need to keep coming back to them to find out more.

Here is a man enjoying all the riches and rewards that life has to offer. Without a care in the world, he can plan ahead with confidence and suck the marrow of a very comfortable life. It is at this very moment, though, with his future secure, that he dies. The heart of life lies in seeking the presence and the purposes of God in each moment, so that we store up lasting treasure and learn to sit lightly to the so-called treasures of the world.

Generous God, reveal your presence in each moment of my life, that I may store up treasure in heaven.

STEPHEN COTTRELL

Seek first the kingdom

Luke 12:22, 24–25, 27–31 (NRSV, abridged)

[Jesus] said to his disciples, 'Therefore I tell you, do not worry about your life, what you will eat, or about your body, what you will wear... Consider the ravens: they neither sow nor reap, they have neither storehouse nor barn, and yet God feeds them. Of how much more value are you than the birds! And can any of you by worrying add a single hour to your span of life?... Consider the lilies, how they grow: they neither toil nor spin; yet I tell you, even Solomon in all his glory was not clothed like one of these. But if God so clothes the grass of the field... how much more will he clothe you – you of little faith! And do not keep striving for what you are to eat and what you are to drink, and do not keep worrying. For it is the nations of the world that strive after all these things, and your Father knows that you need them. Instead, strive for his kingdom, and these things will be given to you as well.'

Reflection

In the light of this wisdom – that we can dwell in God's presence and find there our security and affirmation – we come now to this important passage, where Jesus, pointing to God's created order, shows how it, too, reveals God's wisdom and provision. As the psalmist puts it (Psalm 19:1), 'The heavens are telling the glory of God; and the firmament proclaims his handiwork.'

The ravens do not sow. They do not even own barns – like the rich man in yesterday's story, who looked for security in his own wealth – but they are still fed. The lilies, too, do not spin, but they are still wonderfully clothed. Likewise, we do not need to strive for food or security: 'Give us our daily bread' is the only prayer that we need. Instead, we must seek God's kingdom – 'your will be done' – and then everything else will be added.

What is this kingdom? It is not measured by boundaries of time or space. It is about living under the rule of God – that just and gentle rule inaugurated in Christ.

Lord Jesus, show us your kingdom.

STEPHEN COTTRELL

A new heart

Luke 12:32–34 (NRSV)

'Do not be afraid, little flock, for it is your Father's good pleasure to give you the kingdom. Sell your possessions, and give alms. Make purses for yourselves that do not wear out, an unfailing treasure in heaven, where no thief comes near and no moth destroys. For where your treasure is, there your heart will be also.'

Reflection

When Jesus was born, wise men came to visit him, symbol-ising the wealth and wisdom of the world bending the knee before what God was doing in Jesus Christ. Wise people still find their way to Christ, and those who wish to be wise sit at his feet. When we do this, he gives us his kingdom. We are not just citizens of this kingdom but also, with Christ, co-heirs (Romans 8:17).

The values of this kingdom seem odd to the world. They demand a new set of relationships – not just with God and with each other but also with the planet itself and all the possessions that we have hitherto considered so important. We must not only sit lightly to the things of the world but also walk lightly on the surface of the earth. First, because it is not ours to do with as we wish and, second, because our true home is with Christ himself. This is the unfailing treasure of heaven. It requires a purse that will not wear out, one that no burglar can pinch. Such a purse is made of those attitudes and values that we see lived so abundantly in Christ, which we now seek, by the working of the Holy Spirit, to inculcate in ourselves. Above all, it involves an open heart, ready to receive from God. As Proverbs puts it, 'Keep your heart with all vigilance, for from it flow the springs of life' (4:23).

We need not fear. More than anything else, that is what God wants to give us – a new heart. It is the Father's good pleasure to draw us into new and loving relationships and for us to draw from him the kindly wisdom that changes the world.

**Bountiful God, give me a new heart, and lead me
to the wisdom of Christ.**

STEPHEN COTTRELL

The last shall be first

Luke 12:35–38 (NRSV)

'Be dressed for action and have your lamps lit; be like those who are waiting for their master to return from the wedding banquet, so that they may open the door for him as soon as he comes and knocks. Blessed are those slaves whom the master finds alert when he comes; truly I tell you, he will fasten his belt and have them sit down to eat, and he will come and serve them. If he comes during the middle of the night, or near dawn, and finds them so, blessed are those slaves.'

Reflection

We finish where we started, with a story about someone being served at table. We are told that we must be like faithful servants who are waiting for the master's return, who are ready to serve him as soon as he comes knocking at the door. We are to be both Martha and Mary, attentive to Jesus and ready to serve him. Then there is a twist – one so subtle that I expect many people have read this little story many times and not even noticed it. The master returns; the servants are ready, dressed for action, with their lamps lit. In the upside-down economy of the kingdom of God, however, the tables are turned. The master returns all right, but, instead of sitting down and receiving their service, *he waits on them*! It is an astonishing turnaround: the master becomes an attentive Mary and a bustling Martha. He fastens his belt, sits the servants down and serves *them*.

Who but a God who eats with sinners, washes feet and welcomes strangers could tell such a story? God serves us in the kingdom where the first are last and the humble lifted high. Like the Lord's mother, let us treasure this wisdom in our hearts (Luke 2:51) and live it all our days.

Merciful God, I thank you for the service you have shown me in Christ, and for the wisdom you put in my heart. Help me to serve Christ in others, to be attentive to his word, to look for his coming and to live as a child of his kingdom.

STEPHEN COTTRELL

Week 6 | Group study questions

Luke 11:37–41 (Monday)

1 As a group, find out who likes daily routines and structures and who prefers variety. Does this apply in our spiritual lives too?

2 Which Christian rituals or spiritual disciplines do you find helpful or are you interested in exploring?

3 If we were to create a 'rule of life' that helps us 'practise the presence of God', what would it be?

4 Choose one small ritual or habit that you could stop, either for the week or permanently.

5 Choose a ritual to adopt for the week or for the rest of Lent.

1 Corinthians 13

TONY HORSFALL

A much better way

1 Corinthians 12:31b (NIV)

I will show you the most excellent way.

Reflection

The apostle Paul's famous 'hymn to love' in 1 Corinthians 13, so often read at weddings, has to be seen within its context to be properly understood and appreciated.

Taking the epistle as a whole, we note that it is written to the church at Corinth, a church broken by division, poisoned by quarrels, tainted by sin and yet puffed up with spiritual pride. Such a group desperately needed to understand the true nature of Christian love and their responsibility to walk in that love.

Its immediate setting is 'sandwiched' between chapter 12, which speaks about the diversity of gifts within the church, and chapter 14, which highlights in particular the use of the gifts of prophecy and speaking in tongues. If the church at Corinth is to enjoy unity within such diversity, and also operate the gifts of the Spirit in a way that edifies the whole congregation, then it must be a church that is soaked in

God's love, where each individual expresses that love in their relationships together.

Paul's beautiful exposition of the nature of godly love is not intended exclusively for couples about to be married. It is a call to Christian congregations to seek a 'most excellent way', the way of love, and become communities of grace. It is easy to settle for the ordinary, mundane, commonly accepted way of living, but Paul calls us on to excellence, to a higher standard where we love each other with the love of Christ. Like a coach who can never be satisfied with a run-of-the-mill performance, he spurs us on to greater things.

What Paul describes here is the 'royal law' (James 2:8), where we learn to love others as ourselves. His summons is to express Jesus' new commandment – that we love one another – in every aspect of our life together (John 13:34). What really matters is that we serve one another in love (Galatians 5:13).

We must beware, though, of trying to love others in our own strength. This kind of love is divine and can only be experienced by the life of Christ working within us.

Lord, make your church a place of love, and show me how to let Christ love through me. Amen

TONY HORSFALL

Without love I am nothing

1 Corinthians 13:1–3 (NIV)

If I speak in the tongues of men or of angels, but do not have love, I am only a resounding gong or a clanging cymbal. If I have the gift of prophecy and can fathom all mysteries and all knowledge, and if I have a faith that can move mountains, but do not have love, I am nothing. If I give all I possess to the poor and give over my body to hardship that I may boast, but do not have love, I gain nothing.

Reflection

Paul begins by reminding us that love is essential. It is a priority, the quality that marks our actions as truly Christian. Everything we do is to be the expression of God's love within our hearts. To the church at Corinth, obsessed with the supernatural and spectacular, he gives a balancing reminder of the importance of doing everything in love.

Love is more important than words. The most eloquent preaching, if devoid of love, will leave its hearers untouched and unmoved. To exercise the gift of tongues (the prayer language of the Spirit) is good and valid, but to do so in self-display and without truly loving others turns our words into empty noise.

Love is more important than wonders. We need the supernatural insight that prophecy can bring and powerful manifestations of the gift of faith but, unless these are operating in the context of love for others, they will be lacking something essential. Indeed, those privileged enough to be used by God in such ways run the risk of becoming proud and conceited unless motivated by love alone.

Love is more important than works. Sacrificial acts of generosity are to be applauded and radical obedience admired, but without love even our works can be unproductive. Good works disassociated from love lead to empty religion and self-righteousness. Only actions born out of God's own compassion carry the seal of his approval.

William Barclay, in his commentary on 1 Corinthians, rightly said that this passage demands much self-examination from the good man or woman. It is important that our Christian activity is motivated by genuine love for others and the desire to edify them, not to bring attention to ourselves or feed our own ego.

**Lord, help me to serve others gladly out of the love
you place in my heart. May I exercise my gifts for
your glory. Amen**

TONY HORSFALL

Love described

1 Corinthians 13:4–6 (NIV)

Love is patient, love is kind. It does not envy, it does not boast, it is not proud. It does not dishonour others, it is not self-seeking, it is not easily angered, it keeps no record of wrongs. Love does not delight in evil but rejoices with the truth.

Reflection

Love is neither sentimental nor theoretical, but for the apostle Paul it is extremely practical. His definition is very simple – love is patient and kind. In this it reflects the way that God deals with us, in his mercy (patiently forgiving us) and grace (kindly giving us what we don't deserve). Those who have received such love can share it freely with others. We can choose to be long-suffering with people who frustrate us, and we can seek, through simple acts of kindness, to demonstrate God's love to others.

The security and acceptance that comes from knowing we are loved unconditionally by God releases us from being envious or jealous at the success of others and frees us from the need to brag or boast of our own achievements. This love in our hearts teaches us to be sensitive to the needs of others, to consider the impact of our words and actions, preventing us from behaving inappropriately.

This same love delivers us from self-centred living, thinking only of our own needs and interests, and liberates us into joyful thoughtfulness for others. It enables us to hold our tongue when provoked, choosing not to retaliate with harsh and cutting words but, rather, control our temper.

Love moves us to forgive when we have been wronged or wounded or hurt. It suffers from short-term memory loss, for it chooses not to keep a record of previous wrongs or to bring them up as a constant reminder of past failures. Having been forgiven ourselves and had our slate wiped clean, we find the freedom to respond to others with forgiving grace.

Love can never delight in the downfall or loss of another, even one who has hurt us. It has been loosed from the chains of revenge or vindictiveness. Now it rejoices in what is good, wholesome and true.

**Lord, my own love is so shallow and fleeting.
Move in my heart today and fill me afresh
with your own perfect love. Amen**

TONY HORSFALL

Covered by love

1 Corinthians 13:7 (NIV)

[Love] always protects, always trusts, always hopes, always perseveres.

Reflection

There is an obvious connection between love and grace. God's unceasing love towards us is expressed in the activity of grace: he gives to us freely a salvation that we could never earn or deserve. He loves us unconditionally, and nothing we could ever do will change his enduring love for us.

Once his love has been established in our own hearts, we are able to love others, too, and show this same grace towards them. This thought lies behind Paul's assertion that love always protects. It provides a covering, a place of refuge and safety for those who have failed and done wrong. Rather than casting them out, it welcomes them back in accepting, non-judgemental love. It offers the freedom of forgiveness.

Love has a way of believing the best about people. Knowing that we are made in the image of God, it sees the worth and value in every individual, however hidden it may be. Love treats them accordingly, with dignity and respect, care and concern. Above all, it dares to trust others and refuses to become cynical or hard-hearted. Of course there is always a risk when we trust others, but that is part of loving.

Love is optimistic. It dares to believe that people can change, that with God's help they can be different. It provides a second chance, an opportunity to start again. It is motivated by faith in the power of God to transform and redeem human lives.

This kind of love has great staying power. It endures. It stays the distance. It is robust and not easily discouraged or put off. It perseveres with people, just as God perseveres with us.

It is this covering love that we see in the father's response to his prodigal son, in the story Jesus told in Luke 15. And it is this same forgiving grace that we see offered by Jesus to the woman caught in the act of adultery (John 8:2–11).

This love waits to move within our hearts too, if we are willing.

Lord, show me today where to spread the cloak of your covering love. Amen

TONY HORSFALL

Love that is eternal

1 Corinthians 13:8–10, 12 (NIV)

Love never fails. But where there are prophecies, they will cease; where there are tongues, they will be stilled; where there is knowledge, it will pass away. For we know in part and we prophesy in part, but when completeness comes, what is in part disappears… For now we see only a reflection as in a mirror; then we shall see face to face. Now I know in part; then I shall know fully, even as I am fully known.

Reflection

If we commit ourselves to love, we will always do the right thing. There will be times when we need to confront situations and speak the truth that challenges others, but even then we can speak with the sensitivity and carefulness of love (Ephesians 4:15). Love never fails.

Behind Paul's thinking in these verses is his conviction that this present life is not all there is. For Christians, the best is yet to be, when Christ returns and establishes his kingdom. This eternal perspective helps us to evaluate things on earth, to distinguish between what is temporary and what is permanent, between the imperfect and the perfect.

Christians must learn to live in the light of eternity. Our lives are governed by the future, not the past, or even the present. Thus, we should not be carried away with the excitement of spiritual gifts. Prophecy, tongues and words of knowledge are spectacular gifts of the Spirit and a great help to us here on earth, but they are temporary and the time will come when they will not be needed.

At present, there are many things we do not understand. We see only dimly, like looking in one of the polished metal mirrors made in Corinth. We experience mystery, enigma and uncertainty here on earth, which is why the gifts of the Spirit are so helpful. They enable us to pierce the darkness a little. When the kingdom of God comes fully, however, all mystery will be gone and we will need them no more.

The one enduring quality is love. It will never pass away or become obsolete. It is the foundation of the coming kingdom.

Lord, help me to have the right perspective and, even in times of perplexity, choose the way of love.

TONY HORSFALL

Growing to maturity

1 Corinthians 13:11 (NIV)

When I was a child, I talked like a child, I thought like a child, I reasoned like a child. When I became a man, I put the ways of childhood behind me.

Reflection

As a teacher, I was often on playground duty, sorting out the squabbles and fights. As a church leader, I feel I'm sometimes called to do the same.

One of the main reasons for the turmoil in the Corinthian church was that many of them were still behaving like children. They had their favourite preachers, wanted their own way and quarrelled endlessly. No wonder Paul rebuked them. 'Brothers and sisters,' he said, 'I could not address you as people who live by the Spirit but as people who are still worldly – mere infants in Christ' (3:1).

Generally speaking, children are almost always selfish and self-centred in their behaviour. 'Me first!' is a common cry. It requires a certain growth and maturity to be able to act outside of one's own self-interest, to be able to put the needs of others before our own. Of course, there are many adults who still behave in childish ways, and such was the situation at Corinth.

The more excellent way that Paul is speaking about here requires one thing – that we leave childish ways behind us and press on to maturity.

In immature hands, the gifts of the Spirit could easily be misused and become divisive. There was a danger that they became toys to play with, rather than tools to build up the body of Christ and further the purposes of God. Hence, Paul insists that they must be used in love, for the edification of everyone, not just the satisfaction of the individual.

Those who are mature in Christ have learned to speak, think and reason in love. The gifts of the Spirit are safe in their hands, for they seek not their own advancement but the blessing of others. They have the maturity to put others first.

It is not easy to arrive at spiritual maturity. We have to put off our childish ways. It is sometimes painful or humbling to recognise our own immaturity and turn from it, but, to find the more excellent way, we must be willing to do so.

Lord, show me where I am being childish, and help me grow up in Christ. Amen

TONY HORSFALL

Only love remains

1 Corinthians 13:13 (NIV)

And now these three remain: faith, hope and love. But the greatest of these is love.

Reflection

Paul's great 'hymn to love' climaxes with the identification of a trinity of qualities often seen together in the New Testament – faith, hope and love.

Faith is our response to God and, without faith, it is impossible to please him (Hebrews 11:6). Faith takes God at his word and believes that what he says is true. Faith is the hand that reaches out to receive what God has provided. We are saved by grace (God's part), but through faith (our response). Moreover, it is faith that helps us to trust God when the way is uncertain. In this life, where we see through a glass darkly, we are called to walk with faith, not by sight (2 Corinthians 5:7).

Hope is more focused on the future and is defined as 'a confident expectation of good that is to come'. We are saved in hope, because many of the blessings of salvation are reserved for the future. We know the reality of forgiveness now and have eternal life, but we await the return of Jesus and all the joys of heaven. We live in the tension of the kingdom having started, but not yet come to completion. We taste the powers of the age to come, but they are not yet fully present, so we wait in hope for all that is yet to be.

Once the kingdom of God has fully come, neither faith nor hope will be needed – faith because we shall see Jesus face-to-face, and hope because all we have longed for will be realised. The one thing that will remain, however, is love.

When the kingdom comes, it will be characterised by perfect love. Not only will we love God perfectly, but we will also have been made perfect in our love for one another. No sin nor immaturity will spoil relationships then. We will dwell in perfect harmony, in total and complete love.

It is good to seek spiritual gifts, but even more important to make love our aim. Love alone will remain. It is the atmosphere of heaven.

Lord, as I anticipate the glory still to come,
keep me strong in faith and hope. Above all, let
my heart be filled with heavenly love. Amen

TONY HORSFALL

Week 7 | Group study questions

1 Corinthians 13:13 (Saturday)

1 Read the whole of 1 Corinthians 13 together. What does this chapter teach us about love?

2 Where would you locate yourself on the path to spiritual maturity – and why? Does your 'rating' relate to your understanding or your behaviour, for example?

3 How can we encourage each other towards spiritual maturity, 'growing up in Christ'?

4 How can we show Christian love as a group: to each other? Within the church? To our wider community?

5 What can we commit to and pray for each other this week?

Luke 22–24: from upper room to Easter Day

BROTHER RAMON SSF

My body, my blood

Luke 22:14–19 (NRSV)

When the hour came, he took his place at the table, and the apostles with him. He said to them, 'I have eagerly desired to eat this Passover with you before I suffer; for I tell you, I will not eat it until it is fulfilled in the kingdom of God.' Then he took a cup, and after giving thanks he said, 'Take this and divide it among yourselves; for I tell you that from now on I will not drink of the fruit of the vine until the kingdom of God comes.' Then he took a loaf of bread, and when he had given thanks, he broke it and gave it to them, saying, 'This is my body, which is given for you. Do this in remembrance of me.'

Reflection

These words and this account are both simple and sublime. Here, as we approach Holy Week, we are placed by our Lord at his table and open to the words and actions that draw us close to his heart of love. He talks about his eager desire to share the Passover with us and his longing for us to enter more deeply into the compassion that leads him to Calvary.

How difficult it is for us to understand this single, overwhelming passion. If we have glimpsed it in the life of a great musician, artist, poet, scientist – that drive to do one thing, to give oneself completely to one love – then we shall have at least glimpsed what Jesus means.

The disciples were perplexed, the darkness was deepening, Judas was about to leave the company to deliver Jesus into the hands of his murderers. Here, however, Jesus is radiant, with sorrow in their midst, talking about the breaking of his body and the shedding of his blood in suffering in order that he might accomplish that mighty work of salvation on our behalf.

There are times in our lives when we must stay close to our Lord's heart, sharing his suffering in the 'not knowing' attitude of faith. There was much darkness and betrayal before the chosen band, but on the further side there was glory.

Enable me, Lord, to share your darkness, so that you may bring me at last into your eternal light.

BROTHER RAMON SSF

Denial and restoration

Luke 22:31–34 (NRSV)

'Simon, Simon, listen! Satan has demanded to sift all of you like wheat, but I have prayed for you that your own faith may not fail; and you, when once you have turned back, strengthen your brothers.' And he said to him, 'Lord, I am ready to go with you to prison and to death!' Jesus said, 'I tell you, Peter, the cock will not crow this day, until you have denied three times that you know me.'

Reflection

Poor Peter. He had an inordinate estimate of his own ability, strength and courage. In verse 62 of this chapter, after the foretold denial, it states, 'He went out and wept bitterly.'

My father was a good man – he loved me and I him – but, occasionally, he had a half-pint too much with his few friends and became sentimental and maudlin. He came home in such a state one Saturday evening when I was about eleven years old. I was alone and, on sitting down with me, the tears began to flow. I was embarrassed and said, 'What's wrong, Dad?' He said, 'I'm wrong, my son. I've not been a good father to you and I don't bring you up as I ought.' 'Don't be so daft,' I replied, 'you're a perfectly good father to me,' and we both wept together. I could see deeper into his soul than he could – I could see the potential, the warmth and the care that both he and my mother gave me and my baby sister. Even now, my sister and I visit the grave, pray there, chuckle and wonder how we managed to bring up our parents so well!

I'm saying this today because it seems to illustrate our scripture in that Jesus knew well – oh so well – the deficiencies and idiosyncrasies of Simon Peter, but he looked beyond them, beyond the denials, into the areas of restoration, leadership and loving service. The Holy Spirit would not only give him strength to stand against Satan, but also impart discernment and strength in rebuilding and leading the apostolic band.

So it is with our lives. We need the same kind of discernment as we look into our own souls as Jesus had when he looked into Peter's, as I had when I looked into my father's. We also need the simple, trusting faith to weep for our sins, trust in Christ's love and receive of his Spirit.

Lord Jesus, look deep into my soul, make your diagnosis, prescribe for my needs and grant me the medicine of your forgiving love and power.

BROTHER RAMON SSF

'No more of this!'

Luke 22:47–51 (NRSV)

Suddenly a crowd came, and the one called Judas, one of the twelve, was leading them. He approached Jesus to kiss him; but Jesus said to him, 'Judas, is it with a kiss that you are betraying the Son of Man?' When those who were around him saw what was coming, they asked, 'Lord, should we strike with the sword?' Then one of them struck the slave of the high priest and cut off his right ear. But Jesus said, 'No more of this!' And he touched his ear and healed him.

Reflection

Only John's gospel names Peter as the swordsman, because by then it was safe to do so. However, the question, 'Should we strike with the sword?' ought not to have been asked. Jesus replied with the words 'No more of this!' and with his healing action. However, drawn down through the ages, the church has continued to ask that question, has not listened to the gospel and has continued to use the sword of violence in all manner of ways.

Indeed, the three great faiths of Judaism, Islam and Christianity have produced their holy wars, jihads and crusades, together with a theological and logical justification for them. I had a sad exchange with a gentle Hindu consultant in Kidderminster hospital. He talked about the way in which, for centuries, Christians, Hindus and Muslims have lived in his part of India amicably, but that, in more recent years, political ferment has produced and stimulated violence between such religious people. Fear is its basis, and the less these religious people now relate in warmth and common sharing, the less they understand one another. The less they understand one another, the more they fear one another, and so the vicious circle is produced.

Let us stand with Jesus in Gethsemane today. Let us listen to his gospel teaching. Let us put into practice his pattern of non-violence. How can we do this? By first of all living the Christ-life and, as a result of that, sharing with our neighbours of other faiths and none. For they also have reasons for the hope that lies within them. Then, as a result of such an attitude on our part, we shall stimulate sympathy and understanding on theirs – like my Hindu consultant friend.

Let there be enough of physical violence, mental superiority, pride and conceit. Teach me humility, Lord, at all levels of my life.

BROTHER RAMON SSF

I will release him

Luke 23:13–16 (NRSV)

Pilate then called together the chief priests, the leaders, and the people, and said to them, 'You brought me this man as one who was perverting the people; and here I have examined him in your presence and have not found this man guilty of any of your charges against him. Neither has Herod, for he sent him back to us. Indeed, he has done nothing to deserve death. I will therefore have him flogged and release him.'

Reflection

That really was Pilate's hope and intention. He had his external evidence before him, his internal conscience to convict him and people like his wife to warn him. Despite all these things, within the next few verses Pilate releases the criminal Barabbas and hands over Jesus to be flogged and crucified. What a turnabout!

We are now in the middle of Holy Week. I remember that, during my time on the staff of St Mary's Episcopal Cathedral, Glasgow, Holy Week was marked with an especial reverence – a kind of living in two worlds at once. For me, it was that strange and wonderful sacredness that pervaded the cathedral, with its purple covering over statues, pictures and sacred art, and the way it affected my thinking, living and speaking in busy Glasgow during those days leading up to Easter.

For Pilate, it was Jesus shrouded in purple, crowned with thorns, bearing the pretentious symbols the soldiers had put into his hands that caused him to halt in his steps and *want* to release him. The crowd, though, was too much, the herd instinct too great, the threat too terrifying. He gave in at the last, so his name is enshrined in the Apostles' Creed as causing Christ's suffering. He could have stood his ground and made one glorious decision that would have turned the course of his life. On such confrontations as these hangs our eternal salvation.

Today, as we go forward together into the next few days of reflection, let us become aware of the way in which Pilate's decision started the wheels of the crucifixion turning and drew so many into the events that led to both the darkest darkness and the most wondrous light. We, too, are involved, for it is our journey as well as theirs.

Lord Jesus, I am moved by the crowd. Let me be more deeply moved by your Spirit and stand with you.

BROTHER RAMON SSF

'They do not know what they are doing'

Luke 23:32–35 (NRSV)

Two others also, who were criminals, were led away to be put to death with him. When they came to the place that is called The Skull, they crucified Jesus there with the criminals, one on his right and one on his left. Then Jesus said, 'Father, forgive them; for they do not know what they are doing.' And they cast lots to divide his clothing. And the people stood by, watching; but the leaders scoffed at him, saying, 'He saved others; let him save himself if he is the Messiah of God, his chosen one!'

Reflection

The prayer of Jesus lightens the darkness of this scene. How is it possible that, at the beginning of this mortal agony, with the desolate anguish of death by crucifixion before him, Jesus can pray for his crucifiers with a forgiveness that passes our understanding? As Bishop Ryle said, there was one dying thief redeemed so that none need despair, but *only* one, that none may presume. Yet Jesus spread his covering love of forgiveness over all those who acted in ignorance, from plain duty or because they simply did not know who he was or what was going on.

There are times when Jesus' covering love surrounds us in this way. He 'covers' those who are born with disabilities in their mind or body, those who are caught up in society's mismanagement of their lives, those who strive all their lives to live in love and constantly fall because of the wickedness and scheming of evil enemies.

They have only to exercise that faint action of faith or hope in his goodness and love; they have only to reckon on his forgiving mercy; they have only to believe that he wills to help and save them. 'Father, forgive them,' he repeats – and that prayer is uttered down the centuries, among the nations, and will at last become the reverberating sound of victory that accompanies his last victorious cry, 'It is finished!' (John 19:30).

Lord Jesus, when I do not know what I am doing, bring me to my senses, let me affirm your suffering love and do your good and perfect will.

BROTHER RAMON SSF

'Father, into your hands'

Luke 23:44–47 (NRSV)

It was now about noon, and darkness came over the whole land until three in the afternoon, while the sun's light failed; and the curtain of the temple was torn in two. Then Jesus, crying with a loud voice, said, 'Father, into your hands I commend my spirit.' Having said this, he breathed his last. When the centurion saw what had taken place, he praised God and said, 'Certainly this man was innocent.'

Reflection

I remember asking my mother when I was about ten years old why it was called 'Good Friday', not 'Bad Friday', and she replied that something good came out of it. It is an amazing fact that we have a faith at the centre of which such words of affirmation can be repeated in our dying hours: 'Father, into your hands I commend my spirit.' How good this Friday is!

Whatever happens to me in this dark and violent world, whatever tragedy, sickness or catastrophe may overcome my life or family, whatever personal pain and grief may come my way, I can commend my spirit to my heavenly

Father in confident trust for eternity. Thus, this black today can become for me 'Good Friday'.

I make my way to the house of God with my fellow believers today, to weep with them, to rejoice with them, to enter into that covenant of love with them within the love of God, because it is 'Good Friday'. I know that this Good Friday will usher me into Holy Saturday and the world will soon be filled with the new dawn of Easter Day, when the whole cosmos will be filled with the resurrection of the Lord Jesus.

He was put to death on Good Friday, but I rejoice today and mingle my tears with his joy, and his tears with my glory. We can do this together, for it is a covenant relationship of love for the covenant people of God.

If my light fails, my sun darkens and the veil of my life is torn in two, you are here for me, Lord, for it is Good Friday. I wait on you for further revelation of your love in the silence.

BROTHER RAMON SSF

Saturday of stillness

Luke 23:50–54 (NRSV)

Now there was a good and righteous man named Joseph, who, though a member of the council, had not agreed to their plan and action. He came from the Jewish town of Arimathea, and he was waiting expectantly for the kingdom of God. This man went to Pilate and asked for the body of Jesus. Then he took it down, wrapped it in a linen cloth, and laid it in a rock-hewn tomb where no one had ever been laid. It was the day of Preparation, and the sabbath was beginning.

Reflection

If the Friday has a claim to be called 'Good', this day has a claim to be called 'Holy', 'Silent', 'Tranquil' or 'Still'. It possesses the most wonderful sense of silent stillness, different from any other day of the year. The suffering, darkness and pain of Good Friday are over, together with its grieving and flurried activity, as this righteous man has brought the body of Jesus into the stillness of his garden tomb. Then, there is the holiness, the silence, the waiting.

There is traditionally no celebration of the Eucharist on this day, no receiving of Holy Communion. The day is simply given over to a blessed waiting – and it is blessed because it has that fragrant warmth about it that is full of spring and Easter promise. The very world of nature holds its breath and all the fresh flowers and buds of the season seem about to burst into a glory that never can be expressed, save in what happens tomorrow – and it will happen! There is no doubt now, for this is Holy Saturday, and we are waiting.

As we wait, let us cultivate before our Lord that blessedness of anchoring ourselves into this Holy Saturday stillness, so that it may become a mark and pattern of our lives. For then, every day will contain elements of such stillness that will be cherished by us and communicated to those around us.

**Lord Jesus, into the still silence of this day
may your glory shine.**

BROTHER RAMON SSF

Jesus himself stood among them

Luke 24:36–40 (NRSV)

While they were talking about this, Jesus himself stood among them and said to them, 'Peace be with you.' They were startled and terrified, and thought that they were seeing a ghost. He said to them, 'Why are you frightened, and why do doubts arise in your hearts? Look at my hands and my feet; see that it is I myself. Touch me and see; for a ghost does not have flesh and bones as you see that I have.' And when he had said this, he showed them his hands and his feet.

Reflection

There was no doubt about it. He was not a ghost, yet he did not simply have a resuscitated physical body, carrying all the marks of frail mortality. He had a glorious and spiritual body, for mere flesh and blood cannot inherit the kingdom of God. This body had left the tomb, possessing Jesus' crucified body, spiritualising and energising it with such immortal glory that we cannot begin to imagine it. He was not a ghost, but no wonder they were terrified!

Today, we are full of unspeakable joy and full of glory. Today, Christ is risen from the dead and becomes our glorified and exalted Saviour. Today, Jesus reveals himself to his disciples and prepares to enter again that eternal heavenly realm from which he will bless and lead his church into the blessing of the Holy Spirit and to await his eventual coming in glory.

The wonder of it all proceeds from the eternal fountain of God's love, flows into our dark and sinful world for our redemption and flows back to the eternal fruitfulness of God the Father, to whom be praise and glory on this resurrection day – and forever! Amen!

Heavenly Father, may the resurrection glory dwell in our hearts today, and let us rejoice in the power of your Holy Spirit.

BROTHER RAMON SSF

Week 8 | Group study questions

Holy Week

1 Describe your celebration of Easter this year.

2 How would you describe what Easter means to you if somebody asked you?

3 For whom can we pray for Easter resurrection, hope and healing?

4 What can you carry forward from these Lenten studies and make a regular part of daily life?

5 Close in prayer and thanksgiving for the miracle of Easter.

Next steps

We have reached Easter Sunday, the climax of our Lenten journey. However, we have not yet arrived at our real destination, because although we have studied and read and reflected and practised for over 40 days, we are not at the very end. The wonder of the empty tomb must continue to send its echoes into our daily lives, as we take up the message it sings to us and sing it in our turn, accompanying our journey with the hymns of redemption and the choruses of salvation. The journey of faith is as long as the journey of our lives, ending only when we arrive at our eternal home, prepared so lovingly for us by Christ, who has gone before us for that very purpose.

Hopefully, the practices of Lent, the disciplines of daily study and reflection, and the structures of prayer and contemplation will have been put in place and, through the steady repetition of the last 40 days, will have become a habit, part of the fabric of our daily lives. However, it is not enough merely to establish a habit – that habit must be kept up if it is to accomplish its purpose.

As we continue beyond Easter, we look for the promises of Pentecost and take upon ourselves the great commission as we continue to explore all that the suffering, death and resurrection of Christ mean for us and for the world.

My prayers are for you as you continue on your journey.

Questions for the next stage of the journey

- What have I learned about myself during this Lenten period?

- What have I learned about God?

- Which spiritual practices have been new to me? How useful have I found them?

- What do I need to do to sustain a practice of prayer and reflection?